Hollywood Irish

To THE HONOURARY

IRISHMAN

GO N'EIRIGH ON BOTHAR LEAT.

Happy Christmas 2001

D1566784

IN THEIR OWN WORDS

ILLUSTRATED INTERVIEWS WITH

gabriel byrne, liam neeson, pierce brosnan, stephen rea, aidan quinn and patrick bergin

Hollywood Irish

EDITED BY ÁINE O'CONNOR

ROBERTS
RINEHART
PUBLISHERS

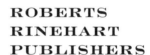

IN THEIR OWN WORDS

Published in the United States and Canada
by Roberts Rinehart Publishers,
5455 Spine Road, Boulder, Colorado 80301
TEL. 303.530.4400

Distributed to the trade by Publishers Group West

ISBN 1-57098-109-4

Library of Congress Card Catalog Number 97-65649

Published in Ireland as *Leading Hollywood*
by Wolfhound Press Ltd.
68 Mountjoy Square
Dublin 1, Ireland

ILLUSTRATED INTERVIEWS WITH
gabriel byrne, liam neeson, pierce brosnan,
stephen rea, aidan quinn and patrick bergin

ACKNOWLEDGMENTS

Thanks to: Trixie Flynn; Ginette Chalmers of Peters, Fraser & Dunlop; Amy Singer; Daria Vogel of Susan Culley & Associates; Roddy Flynn; Baker Winokur Ryder Public Relations; Kitty Neeson; Teri Hayden; Gráinne Humphries; Carmel White; Caroline Dawson Associates; Luke Gibbons; Deirdre McMahon; Catherine Ortiz and Andrea Hirschen at Warner Brothers.

And a special word of thanks to Messrs. Bergin, Brosnan, Byrne, Neeson, Quinn and Rea for giving us so much time and commitment.

Áine O'Connor
Gerry McColgan
1996

ILLUSTRATED INTERVIEWS WITH
**gabriel byrne, liam neeson, pierce brosnan,
stephen rea, aidan quinn and patrick bergin**

CONTENTS

introduction áine o'connor.........9

rea....83

byrne.....13

quinn....65

bergin....101

picture sources....138
filmographies......139

neeson....43

brosnan....121

ILLUSTRATED INTERVIEWS WITH
gabriel byrne, liam neeson, pierce brosnan,
stephen rea, aidan quinn and patrick bergin

ILLUSTRATED INTERVIEWS WITH
gabriel byrne, liam neeson, pierce brosnan,
stephen rea, aidan quinn and patrick bergin

INTRODUCTION
ÁINE O'CONNOR

"What is the stars, Joxer? What is the stars?"
Sean O'Casey, Juno and the Paycock

The stars on this occasion are six leading screen actors, all Irish, who have made Hollywood history by breaking through into big-screen stardom from a small country on the edge of Europe. Patrick Bergin, Pierce Brosnan, Gabriel Byrne, Liam Neeson, Aidan Quinn and Stephen Rea have emerged as international screen stars in an industry traditionally dominated by the home team of American leading men. The book Hollywood Irish *and the associated TV documentary series in Ireland,* Leading Hollywood, *celebrates their collective achievement as an important cultural milestone, signaling yet another aspect of Ireland's move onto the international scene in the world of film.*

In this context, the actors have given the fullest and frankest interviews of their careers. In Hollywood Irish, *they offer us unprecedented glimpses of their childhood memories; the pathways which led them to stardom; their experiences of love and loss, marriage and fatherhood; the thrills and the dangers of the Hollywood lifestyle; their views on acting and their advice to aspiring actors; and the most transformative, the most difficult or simply the most embarrassing moments of their careers. Liam Neeson reveals how he considered leaving acting and how he found the confidence to continue; Pierce Brosnan, simply and openly, shares the painful story of his wife Cassie's death; Stephen Rea discusses the relationship between acting and politics; Aidan Quinn talks about the Irish identity and its many paradoxes; Patrick Bergin reveals the temptations of an actor's life and the difficulties of doing love scenes; Gabriel Byrne tells us about the risks and illusions that surround fame.*

These six actors continue a long tradition of Irish leading men in Hollywood—Errol Flynn, James Cagney, Gregory Peck, Richard Harris. . . . They may have very different qualities, yet they have a lot in common: they are men's men, but their tough exteriors are tempered by the sensitivity and vulnerability which are essential to all the greatest heroes of fact or fantasy. The result: men identify with them and women adore them.

Collectively, the six actors represent the flowering of Ireland's post-colonial culture, which is beginning to express its identity on the big screen. Individually, they embody various aspects of the emergence of Ireland since the foundation of the State. The twenty-six counties were declared a Republic in 1948; these six men grew up as the young nation was moving through the events which would shape the modern Irish identity. Stephen Rea, a Northern Irish Protestant, and Liam Neeson, a Catholic from Ballymena, both grew up under partition, in the context of the Troubles. Aidan Quinn—born in the U.S.A. to Irish parents, brought back to Ireland for some of his boyhood, finally settling in the U.S.—is Irish and American at the same time, with all the conflicts that entails. Gabriel Byrne, whose Dublin upbringing was heavily influenced by his family's rural background, was shaped by the cross-fertilization between city

and country in the move towards urbanization in the 1950s. Patrick Bergin—son of a radical union organizer who later became a Labour senator—grew up amidst the struggles of the Labour movement, which have continued since James Connolly in 1916 to the present day. Pierce Brosnan represents the Irish immigrant experience in Britain: like many an Irishman and Irishwoman, he was taken to Britain at a young age and grew to adulthood there.

These men have another thing in common: in their different ways, they all have a very strong sense of their Irish identity. In the dream machine that is the film industry, they have managed to hold on to that, and that is what

they show us on the big screen: the truth of who they are. That is what star quality is— and perhaps that is what Ireland has given them.

ILLUSTRATED INTERVIEWS WITH
gabriel byrne, liam neeson, pierce brosnan,
stephen rea, aidan quinn and patrick bergin

IN THEIR OWN WORDS

ILLUSTRATED INTERVIEWS WITH
gabriel byrne, liam neeson, pierce brosnan,
stephen rea, aidan quinn and patrick bergin

gabriel byrne

was interviewed in Butterfield's—a tiny pub in Ballitore, a small village in County Kildare—where he tasted his first pint of stout in the company of his father, Dan.

IN THEIR OWN WORDS

BEGINNINGS

I was born in the Rotunda Hospital, which is in Dublin, at about three o'clock in the morning. I don't remember very much about it, but the Rotunda Hospital is beside a theatre, and maybe that was fortuitous.

MEMORIES

My very first memory is of being with my mother when she was collecting my younger brother from the hospital. It was a windy day, I remember, and the blanket that he was wrapped in kept flapping in his face, and I remember standing outside the hospital waiting for somebody to collect us.

The next memory that I have is of trying to poison my brother with a bottle of turpentine, which was used for removing wallpaper from the wall. He was in the pram in the front room, alone with me, and he asked for this liquid in a little whiskey bottle, and I gave it to him. He downed a fair bit of it before my father rushed into the room and became quite agitated, and my mother was called to the scene, and then a doctor arrived with a little black bag. My brother and the room smelled of turpentine and vomit. And I remember being chastised and severely reprimanded. I was sitting in the window watching the doctor going out the gate with his little black bag, and my father told me to get out of the window, I wasn't a cat. . . . My brother laughs about it now, but later I did try to choke him with a piece of turnip, which he thought was an apple, and again he turned blue, and there were

Butterfield's pub, in Ballitore, where the interview took place.

"One of the things I was very conscious of, growing up here, was that everybody had some kind of a story. We would come into the pub at night and listen to people sit by the fire and tell stories. . . . When I read certain novels, I place them in my head here, and when I remember Ireland, this village is what I remember."

more scenes of agitation. I had become known as a danger to young life, so I was never allowed to be in the same room as my brother again unattended.

We get on great now, really great. Mind you, he still insists on having the door open any time we're in the house together, just in case.

FAMILY

There were six of us in my family, three boys and three girls, and we lived in a kind of uneasy toleration of each other, as I think most big families do. My sister died about four years ago, at a very young age, so that leaves five of us altogether.

I think the eldest in the family always gets the job of looking after the younger people, so I did that. . . . I remember a TV thing called *The Old Curiosity Shop*, which used to run on BBC; there was an actor in that called Patrick Troughton, who later became Doctor Who and who made a huge impression on me as Quilp. He had long black hair, and was unshaven, and he had a hump. I used to run up and down the stairs at home terrifying my brothers and sisters, who'd scream and say, "Oh no, here comes Quilp!" That was my first performance, if you like. Pathetic but true.

I only knew my paternal grandmother and grandfather through what my father told me about them. We had pictures of them, but I never really had much to do with them. They were very simple farming people. There were tales told that once upon a time they owned vast tracts of land, and they were disinherited and disenfranchised, and sent to wander the roads; but I don't know whether that's true or not. They were simple farming people, farm laborers.

My father was one of five, six people in the family; he became a soldier, and then when he left the army he became a laborer in Guinness's brewery.

While he was working at Guinness's, my mother was at home looking after us. We lived in Drimnagh, on the Brandon Road—it was called after a mountain; all the roads around where we lived were called after mountains, for some reason I never quite understood. There was Brandon, Lissadell, Madigan, Comeragh. . . . We moved from there in a

rainstorm. I remember my mother pushing the pram with my brother inside, and I remember walking up the Walkinstown road towards the mountains. Occasionally these blue lights would flash out of a window, and I asked my mother what they were, and she said they were television sets. I'd never actually seen a television set light up a room before and turn the room blue.

We came to the house, which was at the end of a road leading to the mountain. On that road there were farms, and all these farms and fields eventually led to a little village called Tallaght, where there was an ancient monastic settlement.

There were people there who had all kinds of weird occupations— there was a swill man, I remember.

Gabriel (standing) and his younger brother.

People said he had been disappointed in love, and now he lived with his mother. He was a very sad-faced man who collected swill from the houses to feed the pigs. And there was a man who lived in a ruined castle, which stood on the top of a hill like a black tooth, with his dog. He was known as "the Sack Man" because he dressed completely from head to toe in sacks—tailored sacks that said "Bagnelstown Flour Mills." He had a little hat made out of a sack, and shoes made out of a sack. And then there were a group of men who I think were gypsies—they were called the Bottom Boys and used to ride bicycles with no saddles on them. They'd terrify people by riding at great speed, shouting "hup ya boy ya," through the streets. And then there was a woman called Rosie who never stopped talking; she was the terror of the bus, because she'd get on and just say anything that came into her head, which was quite likely to be an obscenity of some sort. She was in total stream of consciousness. The guy who looked after the cinema was a bald man—when the lights would go down he had the silhouette of Alfred Hitchcock, and every night when the lights went down, the entire audience would start to go "De, de de, di di, de de de," which was the theme song from *Hitchcock*, the TV show. It used to drive him crazy, and he would shine his torch around the cinema in a vain effort to get a hundred and fifty people to shut up.

It was a mixture of the urban and the suburban, and the country and the city. And it was really a glorious place to grow up. Now that area is totally covered with estate houses, and all those farms, all those people with strange occupations, all those characters, are gone.

Graduating from University College Dublin in July 1973.

"I had a brilliant teacher there. . . . He gave us a fantastic love of literature . . . and knowledge, and taught us that the acquisition of knowledge in itself was a very desirable thing, that knowledge could be hip and cool."

CHILDHOOD

I don't really remember what kind of a young fella I was; but I know that there was a picture taken of me in school, with about forty kids, and I was the only one who was smiling. I had my head to one side and I was smiling. So I don't remember childhood as being particularly miserable, and I don't remember it as being particularly happy. I remember miserable incidents, and happy incidents, but I don't think anybody really has a continuously carefree, happy childhood.

In the same way, I was a combination of the extrovert and the introvert. I didn't like being the center of attention. I was sent at a very young age to learn how to play the accordion—an eccentric with a pipe and cravat taught me the rudiments of the accordion, and I then got a job in my uncle's pub playing the four songs that I knew for twelve and sixpence a night. And I hated it; I hated being singled out for any kind of public attention at all. Learning to play "Kelly the Boy from Killane" or "The Bridges of Paris" and having to lug an accordion case around the streets of Dublin while all my friends were playing football or Cowboys and Indians was always a source of tremendous humiliation to me.

SCHOOL

I went to the nuns first of all, in a place called the Coombe, which is a very old part of Dublin. I was taught there by a very elderly nun in a starched white costume with a white headdress which had the effect of framing her face into a kind of ghostly visage. She terrified me.

On the first day I went in with my mother. We arrived at the schoolyard and I saw all these kids running around in new uniforms. . . . I remember seeing a nun go over to a boy and take him by the ear and put him standing in line; and I didn't know that I had to join that line, that I had to go into that school. And suddenly my mother wasn't standing there; I was in this room with this woman dressed in black, with a rosary and a big, long belt hanging from her waist, who was speaking in what I thought was an unkind and unsympathetic voice. And that was the beginning of the fear. I couldn't understand what I was doing there; nobody had explained the concept of school. You just woke up one day and found you were going to school, in a uniform that itched you and in a class that was full of strangers.

At school I kept my eyes down, and I was extremely deferential to teachers and to Brothers, because I realized that on any whim they could really hurt you. I learnt silence and cunning in relation to authority figures at a very early age. We're very enlightened now about corporal punishment in schools, but when I think back on how it was meted out indiscriminately for sometimes imagined offenses . . . It was a tremendously cruel system of discipline. I remember being terrified of these people, with their enormous hands and bullet heads, knowing that if you displeased them in any way you could end up in great pain. And I hated them. To this day I don't have any great love for the Christian Brothers. I couldn't contemplate doing to a child what some of them did.

I'm not saying this out of self-pity—I look back on those days and sometimes I hear people say, "Yes, I experienced the same thing," and they say, "Well, it didn't do us any harm." But I always say that I don't believe it did me any good either. I believe you can get children to learn and to be curious about the world by encouragement, rather than by hitting them with a stick and teaching them through fear. I'm glad that world has gone, I really am. I don't see any benefit to it at all. I lived my schooldays in abject fear. Monday mornings were . . . I still wake up with a part of my brain saying, "I don't have to go to school today, I don't have to go to the Brothers." I've met some of these guys since, and they're basically just men who are forced to live an unnatural celibate lifestyle teaching young boys.

BALLITORE

Ballitore is the place where I grew up in the summers in Ireland. It's a village, about an hour from Dublin, and it's bypassed by all the main roads, so it's preserved a lot of the characteristics that other villages have lost over the years. It's full of history—it was originally a Quaker town, and there's an old mill here that has existed for several centuries. And during the Famine times, there was a great deal of death in Ireland—in 1842 the population was, I think, eight and a half million, and by the end of the Famine, which began in 1845 and ended in 1847, the population had been reduced to four and a half million people; people died or emigrated because of starvation. But Ballitore was lucky because of its Quaker influence and because of the mill. If the mill hadn't been here, perhaps I wouldn't be here, because all my people depended on this mill, and on the generosity of the Quaker settlement here. People were fed, and so they don't have that terrible scar that many towns have—the memory of starvation and death.

The bus used to come from Dublin, and it would come down the hill and stop here. And of course the arrival of the bus every evening was the major event of the day; people would come out of shops to stand and look at who was getting on and who was getting off. There would always be a collection of men in peaked caps smoking cigarettes over by the clock, which was permanently stopped at ten to two. And myself and my brother would always be the object of curiosity, being from the city—they looked upon us as city slickers and Jackeens, which was the country name for people who came from Dublin. But to me this was a magic, fairytale place, because it was the exact opposite in every sense to the city; and I loved the people here because they were extremely friendly, and they had a great sense of humor—a very dry sense of humor, which I've always appreciated. I always felt at home and welcome here.

I stayed with my father's brother and sister. They had a little farmhouse about three miles from this pub. I suppose my parents wanted to get rid of me for the summer, which I can perfectly understand; but I think they also felt it was important that I experience life in the country—my father's people were from down here. And I'm really glad that they did that, because it's something that's remained with me always. It's a funny thing: when I read certain novels, I place them in my head here, and when I remember Ireland, this village is what I remember. It influenced me very much in the writing that I've done; I've tended to set a lot of stuff here. I tend to write about a lot of the

incidents that I heard about, growing up, and perhaps I have tended to romanticize the area.

I fell very easily into the country way of life— it's genetic, I think, my appreciation of that way of life. I loved the different seasons here—I wasn't here just in the summer. I loved the country routine— going to Mass on Sundays, walking down with hundreds of people to Mass in the morningtimes. The visit to the pictures once, twice a week, on Saturdays and Wednesday nights—I saw a lot of famous movies here. The first Hitchcock movie I ever saw, *North by Northwest*, I saw in this town on a bedsheet. The man used to come on a bicycle with the cans of film from Athy, and we would all wait for him there under the clock. And the seats were bus seats, three and sixpence, and the seats at the back were dining-room chairs. But there was a tremendous atmosphere—the movie was always breaking down, and sometimes it would go upside down, and bedlam would break out and people would demand money back, and so forth. . . . But it was a great place to see films. And then we would walk home at nighttime along the roads, discussing the movie. . . . And I used to come to this pub here with my father, and I partook of my first drink—it was a glass of Guinness—when I was about five or six, sitting over there in that corner by the fire. And in the summertime we would take part in all the things that happened on the farm, like the cutting of the hay. . . .

I've always loved the landscape around here; it's my favorite type of landscape, which is pastoral—the fields are green and yellow, and it really is like a quilted patchwork. There are no high mountains, the sea is far away, but there are rivers and trees and meadows, and sleepy villages like this one. I find that kind of landscape very relaxing. I was stolen by gypsies once. Yeats has a poem called "The Stolen Child"—"Come away . . . to the waters and the wild, with a fairy, hand in hand, for the world's more full of weeping than you can understand," something like that. . . . I remember I was warned by several people not to have anything to do with the gypsies, and of course I didn't pay any attention to them. Then one day this man and his wife, gypsies, pulled up in a horse and cart and asked me if I wanted a lift home, and they seemed to be very nice people and I said yes, and all I can remember is galloping past my house with my father and mother and aunts standing aghast as I was galloped away to captivity. They found me at the turn of the road, anyway, walking back from where these people had let me out. But I was known thereafter as "the boy who was nearly stolen by the tinkers."

One of the things that I was very conscious of, growing up here, was that everybody had some kind of a story. We would come into the pub at night and listen to people sit by the fire and tell stories, and then we would walk home—which was about four miles away—through the dark, terrified by hearing stories about other-worldly creatures and supernatural beings that of course really did exist. And I believed at nighttime I could hear the Headless Horseman who was supposed to ride from Monasterevin to Mullaghmast, an ancient rath, or burial place, near where we lived, every seven years. I would ask foolish questions like "How can he see where he's going, if he has no head?" and people would say "That's not the point, he's a headless horseman."

Then when somebody died you would hear the footsteps walking around the house. . . . And then there was the banshee, who was a ghostly fairy woman who followed certain families whose names began with O, or Mac. Originally our name was O'Byrne, so the banshee followed our family. And

my mother swears that she heard the banshee several times during her life. She would stand outside the house, with her long red hair and a comb, and would comb her hair—the banshee, that is, not my mother!

You grew up there with a very thin line between the natural world and the supernatural world, and the crossover between them happened very frequently, so often you didn't quite know what was the real world and what was the supernatural world. You grew up with a great fear of ghosts and goblins, witches and spirits, and especially of the dead, who would come back to haunt the living or to generally disturb them in some way.

There was a story told that various Irish warriors were lured into Mullaghmast Rath and massacred there by the English, many centuries ago, and of course their ghosts populate the area. Under the rath in Mullaghmast sleep the Red Branch Knights, who are supposed to rise up as one, on the day that Ireland gains its freedom. What they're supposed to do when they rise up I don't know, but they've been asleep for two thousand years so I imagine the first thing they'll do is have a good stretch. . . . My father said to me once that these roads were so full of ghosts that there was hardly room for humans to walk. It was a very naive, primitive, pagan view of the world, and it coexisted with Catholicism. It made for a very unusual world-view.

SPORT

I was very interested in football, Gaelic football. I used to write away to various footballers for their photographs, and I still have pictures at home of fellas in Kerry jerseys and long shorts with their arms folded, "Best wishes" written on them. All my heroes at the time were footballers. I still listen to football matches every Sunday. To me the Sunday-afternoon football match, with Mícheál Ó hEithir commentating, is so resonant. Even when you weren't at home, when you were at the beach maybe, the cars would have their doors open and you could hear the match coming out.

I remember that in football I always followed the underdog—teams like Leitrim and Wicklow that never had a chance of getting to the All-Ireland final. And it's really gratifying to me that recently Leitrim actually got into the All-Ireland semi-final, because I've always supported it—a county I have no connection with whatsoever, except I liked the fact that it has the smallest coastline in Ireland, and that it has no hope whatsoever of ever getting anywhere. My philosophy was that any eejit can support a winning team, but it was great to follow a side that had no hope, and watch them come up. I used to do that in the English divisions as well—I used to support Hartlepool and York City, at the bottom of the fourth division.

I never really was good at hurling; I always found that I was too much of a sissy for hurling, really. But soccer I came to really love, because I had been to school in England, and I followed it. For a while I played football for a Dublin club called Lourdes Celtic. I was a goalkeeper, and I loved playing in goal. I moved out of playing in goal when I got my nose broken for the second time. I had broken it when I was nine; I ran around the

"I want to be remembered as a great father, as a good friend, and as somebody who took chances, who tried to do things that were different."

corner and straight into some girl, who probably has the scars of it today. She smashed my nose, and I think I smashed something of hers—we were both brought to the hospital anyway. And then I broke it as a footballer, and then I broke it again.

I hoped to join the League of Ireland, and I went away to England for trials, which I found totally miserable. . . . Basically my career ended when I discovered girls and cigarettes. That was it for me. Football's loss was the bar-room's gain.

THE MOVIES

I think that the movies were incredibly important to me at the time. I used to go as often as I possibly could—three, four, five, six times a week sometimes. To be in a darkened room, to be by yourself yet to be part of a crowd, to have these worlds beyond imagination opened up to you, and then to come out of those movies fired with imagination and excitement, and to ride nonexistent horses up the road, slapping yourself on the backside, pretending it was a horse . . .

I remember seeing a movie called *Terror in a Texas Town*—I think Sterling Hayden was in it. For months afterwards we re-enacted the entire movie in a field—we knew every line in the film. Then we would do the cowboys thing, and then we did the German concentration camp. I remember one guy who always played the girl—for some reason he was captured with us. He used to wear his sister's pink pullover, and this other guy, playing the camp commandant, would say: "You villt stay heere unt ze girl villt come vit me." The games were full of kind of ambiguous moments like that, but basically we re-enacted what we saw in the movies.

The kind of artistic arguments that used to go on were: who's better, Cliff Richard or Elvis Presley? Cliff Richard was for wimps, and Elvis was for people who knew what the score was. I liked Billy Furey myself—I don't know why, but I did. And somehow I thought that not liking either Elvis or Cliff, and liking Billy Furey, might endear me to some black-haired girl. That was the kind of mad thing going on in my head at the time.

We used to swap these little chewing-gum packets with movie-star faces on them. This guy once said to me, "Do you want to swap Sal Mineo for

With daughter Romy and son Jack.

Audrey Murphy?"

I said, "Who's Audrey Murphy?"

The guy said "Audrey Murphy," and I said, "No, you mean Audie Murphy." And there was a big fight as to whether Audrey Murphy was a girl or Audie Murphy was the war hero from the movie *To Hell and Back*. We knew an awful lot about movies,

With Charlotte Bradley in Draíocht, *the Irish-language film written by and starring Gabriel Byrne and directed by Áine O'Connor.*

but we didn't know an awful lot about movie stars.

I never lost that love of the movies. I used to stand and watch people—the social event of the week at that time was going to the pictures, and so you would watch the guys and the girls walking down at nighttime, click-clacking down the street. And then they would all be up on the balcony, what we used to call "the wearers"—couples who would be kissing and doing things like that. And the thing was to get up to the balcony, to get behind these people and see what in fact they were doing. It reached the stage when the movie became less important than what was going on in the balcony. We would sit behind these couples and be amazed at how the ritual was the same every time. The girl would sit down, the guy would put his arm around her, suddenly the girl would be bent backward, and they would lose total interest in the movie. And the thing was to tap the guy on the shoulder in the middle of this and say, "Scuse me, have you got a light please?"—just to see what his reaction was.

CAREER CHOICES

FROM ALTAR BOY TO SEMINARIAN

I was spending all my time at the movies, but I was also an altar boy, so I went between the two worlds of sanctity and sin. I used to serve Mass; I learned all the Latin, which I really loved the sound of, and which I loved saying. I was addicted at the time to congealed grease—I used to eat the candle grease off the side of the candles—and I used to slug down some altar wine and some hosts. We'd always been told that there were certain things which you should never do: if you went to hit your mother, your hand would wither, and God knows what would happen to you if you ate the host. I never did find out if my hand would wither, but I ate the host and am here to say that nothing happened to me.

I divided the priests into those who said the Mass quick and those who said it slow. There was one priest we used to call Bullet, because he would go through the Mass very quickly. There was another guy—every time he would come out on the altar you could hear a collective sigh from the audience going "Ohhh, not this fella. . . ." This priest—who was very nervous, I remember—had a stammer, and stammered his way through the Mass, so it took forever to get through.

The church was actually a very theatrical place, because what they had to offer, when you think about it, was probably the best theatre show in town. The plainchant was very seductive, and if you inhale incense it has a soporific effect, and there was all the candlelight and flowers. . . . They used the old Latin Mass, where you didn't know what they were saying, and so the mystery of it was also very attractive.

Then I was in school one day, and this man came and showed us slides of where his order had missions—Ecuador, and Bolivia, and Peru. You could see him standing there in a straw hat, tanned, and there were two little black children smiling at the camera, and I thought "I'd like to be there, that looks like a nice place to be." And six months later I found myself on a boat for England, to become a priest. I think I was attracted by the romantic idea of the priesthood, the idea of travel, and the vestments and so forth.

I was eleven and a half. Now, when I think of how young I was, it seems incredible, but I never regretted the experience.

Girls weren't important at that time. If, at the time,

someone had told me all about it and said, "Look, this isn't very important now but in about three or four years' time you're going to notice that girls are on the planet, too," I might have thought twice about it. I'd already fallen in love with a very shy girl in a purple coat, who I never spoke to but saw in the choir in church. I used to gaze at her longingly and lovingly and throw sweet papers at her in the cinema, and ignore her. I had a bike, and once I went down past her house and did some very acrobatic turns on one wheel, in the hope that she might be looking out the bedroom window. If she was, it didn't impress her very much. But I think there's a peculiar thing that happens when you're that age: you think that the object of your affections will come to the window full of concern and say, "Oh God, isn't he unbelievably exciting—the way he's able to do things with that bike. . . . I want to get off with him." I think I still think like that today. I never took the girl out, but she was the fuel for a great deal of fantasy.

In the dormitory of the school in England I was next to a guy from Dublin who had the same name as me—a great guy who was a friend of mine, a great footballer. We used to lie awake at night and discuss all kinds of things. I remember he said to me: "Are you going to get married?" Remember, we were supposed to be studying to be priests, but that didn't seem to me to be a strange question. I said yes, and he said, "What kind of a girl are you going to marry?" I said, "I'm going to marry a girl with dark hair.' I was so sure of this because I'd read *Little Women,* and Beth was the one I really liked. It was kind of the literary equivalent of "Which Beatle do you like?" I liked Beth, and I always imagined that I would marry someone like her, but I never did. The seminary was a wonderful experience.

In a way it was kind of like boarding school, except that the emphasis was obviously on the long-

term hope that these young boys would be turned into priests. It was a great place to be; but it was also a lonely place. When you think of two hundred twelve-year-old boys without mothers or fathers, being looked after by priests . . .

They did have drama there, and I took part. The first time I was ever on stage was in a production of *Oliver!*. Of course I had wanted to play the Artful Dodger. I couldn't sing, but I auditioned as Quilp, playing my old role again. And they said, "No, we don't want that characterization, but you could play a hunchback in a crowd scene." So very early on in the musical, when Oliver is being sold by Mr. Bumble, who sings that song, "Boy for Sale," I came across the stage with a walking stick and my hump, and my Quilp characterization, going "ahahh." I wasn't able to say anything.

I was also the Victor Laudorum 1964—it was an athletic competition where you had to take part in maybe ten different athletic events: the high jump, the long jump, the four-forty, the eight-eighty, the mile, et cetera. . . . The person who won the most events became the Victor Laudorum, which is Latin for "Champion of the Games." I was very physically fit at the time. I think it was just unused sexual energy that propelled me into record-breaking runs; I didn't quite know what else to do with myself.

Gabriel with James Murphy in a scene from Draíocht.

"I've tried to work with the Irish film industry in my own way, by coming back here to do movies. . . . I think it's important that people who achieve a bit of success abroad come back and put something back into the country."

In the end I was drummed out of the seminary. I was called to the rector's office one day, because myself and this chap from Newcastle used to go to the graveyard every morning and smoke three or four Park Drives—they were kind of like Woodbines, except they were just maybe a grade below. We used to smoke these cigarettes in the graveyard, and one day the prefect came into the room and said, "I smell cigarette smoke in the room—if the culprits don't stand up now, the entire class will be. . . ." So we were pointed out as being the culprits, and we were forced to the rector's office. And he said, "Well, I'm really glad you've come to see me, Byrne"—they called you by your second name—"because I've been watching you for quite some time, and it's become extremely apparent to me that you don't have a vocation to the priesthood, and my advice to you is to pack your bags and leave."

So myself and my smoking colleague were brought to Birmingham in a snowstorm and put on a train for London. There was no heat in the carriage, I remember, and at Crewe Station we had to get out and do press-ups on the platform because it was so cold.

I arrived back in Dublin at fifteen and a half or sixteen, exhilarated at being free—and, of course, having discovered that there were girls in the world.

COSTING CLERK

When I first went back to Dublin I became a messenger boy for the firm of Robert J. Jolly & Co, 14-16 Dame Street. I stamped letters, and brought insurance forms from one insurance company to the other, and made the tea, and got things for people for their tea breaks, and stuff like that. And I was really progressing up the ladder there—in fact there was talk of me definitely going into claims, or maybe life assurance if things went well—but I left

to become a costing clerk. And if you knew how bad I was at arithmetic, you'd know that the idea of me becoming a costing clerk was totally ludicrous. I used to hate things in school where they would say, "If it takes three men two weeks to dig a hole five foot long, how long will it take four men to dig the same hole if one of them is X?" I used to look at these things and say, "I don't care how big the hole is, how many of the guys did it. I have no interest whatsoever in the outcome."

But I got a job in the Cosmo Printing House in Capel House, in Dublin, and the theory of ten per cent was explained to me. Ten per cent had to be added on to each bill, and I could never get the concept. I used to just add on ten pounds, or maybe ten shillings sometimes, or maybe four pounds—I'd just take a number and add it on. And I was getting on great, they really liked me there for the first two weeks, till they started getting these irate phone calls from people saying "Hey, my bill came to £425!" And finally it was traced back to me, and Paddy Collins, who was the man who trained me in, said one day, "Look, you're wanted in Mr. Montaine's office at eleven o'clock, for a major talking-to about all this stuff." In the meantime, he said, "Go out and get me ten Craven A." And I never went back. I got out into Capel Street, and I thought, There's no way I can get out of this, so I took Paddy's ten Craven A and I beat it. And I was never seen in Capel Street for years afterwards. In fact every time I go down to Capel Street, I still think Paddy's going to be waiting on the doorstep: "Jaysus, boy, about time."

Now at least I know what the concept of ten per cent is, because my agent at International Creative Management takes ten per cent every time I go to work.

MORGUE ATTENDANT

My mother worked as a nurse in St. Kevin's Hospital in Dublin where she had trained. All of us got jobs there—I worked for a while on the telephones and on the ambulances, and for a very short stint in the morgue. I lasted there maybe a day and a night. It was not what I had set my career hopes on. I'm not great around dead bodies, for a start.

In every job I did there was some kind of an initiation ceremony, which I believe dates back to medieval times and the trade unions and guilds—when you became a plumber, they used to take down your trousers and do unmentionable things with paint and stuff. My brother and other people had warned me to stay calm, that the people in the morgue were going to do something. You'd be there, with the bodies laid out, and of course inevitably one of the bodies would move and you'd hear something go "Oooohhh" under the sheets. I defy anybody to stay calm in a situation like that. You edge gingerly back to the door, thinking, I'm totally calm, this will not get to me—I'll just get out this door now . . . and the door's locked. Great when you're doing it, not so great when you're the victim.

PLUMBER

I then became a plumber, and I was a bit of a disaster at that as well. I was propositioned by an elderly plumber of about seventy, with emphysema, who offered me two and sixpence for a look at my privates.

We used to go on these jobs putting in central heating, and toilets, and so forth, in the cold. It was a miserable existence—rammed into a small toilet with three other plumbers bumping into each other in boiler suits. Eventually someone would say to me, "Would you just get outside, just get out of the toilet, just wait out there." And I was called in again and told that my future did not lie in the plumbing trade and that I should seek employment elsewhere.

UNIVERSITY

I decided that I should go back to school and study for my Leaving Cert. I was quite old at this stage. I fell in love with the idea of being an academic, because I had a brilliant teacher there, a man who had actually retired and come back to teach. This man spoke fluent Latin and Greek, and loved English literature, and used to speak with a kind of halt in his voice: he would sp-eak li-ke th-at, and would talk ab-out Pl-ato. But he gave us a fantastic love of literature, and Latin, and knowledge, and taught us that the acquisition of knowledge in itself was a very desirable thing, that knowledge could be hip and cool.

I took to wearing long coats, and growing my hair; at that time I think I was kind of like Hamlet, with none of the good speeches. I was just morose, wandering around the place alone and palely loitering, being academic and abstracted, because I hoped that—and this is true—there would be a girl somewhere who would say, "See that guy over there in the long coat and the long hair? I know I could go for him." All those things I did were just ruses to get women, really.

Then I got a scholarship to University College Dublin. I was really thrilled, because I had been brought up with the idea that to get to university was a great thing. And I was really proud of the fact that I had gotten to university, still never having passed a maths exam in my life. I'm still useless at arithmetic and maths; I've never in my life passed a maths exam. But I compensated by doing Spanish

Gabriel and costar Ellen Barkin—later his wife—while filming Siesta *in Spain.*

"As soon as you become famous or well-known, a dual reality starts up. Your perception of yourself is one thing, other people's perception of you is another."

and Irish and English, and I got the honors and everything, and I got the grant, and I went and did Irish and Archaeology and Spanish at university.

I spent three years there, basically isolated, dislocated. I didn't have any of those great university times that people talk about; I was very much a loner at the time. I always felt at university that I was in some way not as good as other people. Looking back, it wasn't because of anything other people did; it was me. But it felt like a middle-class environment—it felt elitist, and to me it felt very much like an insiders' club. It made me feel alienated—though again, I think that was all in my own imagination.

I came out with a degree at the end of it. I remember going up the stairs with my father, to accept the scroll, and being met at the top of the stairs by the Registrar and the President—they were just pumping hands with everyone who came up those stairs, and the President congratulated my father on getting his degree. My father turned to him and said, "Jaysus, I barely know how to read and write."

WRITING

I've always been interested in literature, and I've always been interested in writing. While I was at UCD I wanted to do a magazine that blended established writers with young writers. I got J. B. Keane and Ulick O'Connor and Mary Lavin and Christy Brown to write for the magazine, as well as getting younger writers who were at UCD to write poetry and short stories. You had to be an ex-student of UCD; that was the criterion. I edited it and sold it in the pubs around Dublin. It was a bizarre aberration in my life, but I guess everything has a purpose.

I wrote a lot of the stories and some of the poetry in the magazine, under pseudonyms, because we didn't have enough people to fill a couple of issues. I would make up biographies for these pseudonyms: "Seamus MacChommaraigh was born in the Donegal Gaeltacht in 1953, he's at present serving in a ministerial capacity in Ghana," or something.

Liam Nolan was the first person to publish anything that I wrote—he had a radio program called *Here and Now* on RTÉ radio, and he had a short-story slot. The first short story I wrote, called "In Memory of Daffodils," was accepted by him. His producer, a guy called Paddy O'Neill who used to comment on the greyhounds, was in charge of commissioning short stories. I remember getting a letter afterwards from a Professor of English in Cork, called Harry Atkins, who said that I should be a writer. I was twenty at the time. As soon as I got that letter, I thought, Oh my God, and abandoned writing.

The big thing about getting stories on the radio was that it was a major, major event. We'd have a group of friends, I would choose a pub, we'd go there and get the man to put on the radio, and we would listen to the story on the radio, and then get drunk for the rest of the day. But I had a story broadcast on Radio 4, and I can't describe the excitement of the guy saying, "This is the BBC; this morning's story. . . ." And he'd read out the thing and we'd all be sitting in some pub in Ballybrack or wherever, already completely gone with drink—"Oh, ye boy ye. . . ." It would go on for days. It was incredibly exciting.

I've come back to writing recently. It's always been something that I've done—I've kept diaries, and I've always scribbled. But I could certainly get back into it seriously now, with the encouragement of certain people who told me that I could and should do it.

I find writing incredibly difficult—not the actual writing itself, but the getting down to writing. I'll do anything to put it off, and I put it off for years. I'm always afraid that if it comes out of my head onto the paper it will be totally different. It requires tremendous discipline to be a writer, and I'm actually a very lazy person. It requires self-motivation, and self-generation, and I find it very, very difficult to motivate myself, to do something that's only for myself. And also, I'm so in awe of great writers that I find there's a part of me which says I've some cheek to be writing at all.

I've never seriously thought of myself as a writer until the last, I think, year or so. I never accepted that I had any kind of a talent for writing. I'm very doubtful of myself, I never take myself for granted as an actor or producer or writer. I have never felt that I'm in a position where I can be totally at ease with being any of these things. I love doing all these things, but I doubt myself every step of the way.

I write poetry occasionally, but mostly for myself. I find it a very good way of remembering how I felt at a particular time. To me it's like taking a photograph, like sculpting something with words, so that when you look at it in five or ten years' time, you can say, "Yes, I know exactly what that incident was about, I know exactly the significance of it, and I know exactly how I felt at the time." It's my way of taking photographs for myself.

I'm always really pleased with the public reaction to my writing. Dirk Bogarde is an actor I admire greatly who went on to become a writer, and I look at his work and I say, "Well, it's not impossible for me to follow in that way."

TEACHING

After graduating from university I went to Spain to teach. I taught English to bored Spanish housewives, and soldiers in the Spanish army, and young children who were brought by the ear and thrown into rooms with me, and the door locked. I had to teach things like "Rex has the ball. Woof, woof, says Rex," for long afternoons with the sun baking outside, to these women with incredibly long aristocratic fingers and sumptuous rings, all saying to me: "Rex has the ball, woof, woof." I remember saying to fifty soldiers, "So what does Rex say?" and fifty big, macho soldiers, in crew cuts, all saying, "Woof, woof."

I met a girl who always used to say "Ssshh" to me in bars. I'd ask why, and she'd say, "Because everybody in Spain is in the secret service." But three years later, after I'd left Spain, I saw her picture in the newspaper as a woman arrested for the transport of arms. I had a pretty interesting time there.

I went back to Dublin and ended up possibly doing to young kids what had been done to me: I went back to teach Irish and Spanish, in the school where I had graduated. My life became a full circle.

ON STAGE

I was twenty-seven or twenty-eight before I decided to become a full-time actor. I had no idea of becoming an actor when I was living in Spain; it happened when I came back to Dublin. I thought it would be an interesting way of filling up my evenings instead of being in the pub.

I went to the Dublin Shakespeare Society, and I auditioned with all these people who had been in UCD and who all, it seemed to me, spoke in Dublin 4 accents and talked about Shakespeare—"I think

the Merchant is his best play, actually. . . ." I took part in a production of *Coriolanus*, dressed completely in black; I had a black jumper with black bell-bottoms—nobody ever explained how Marcus Aufidius happened to be wearing bell-bottoms in ancient Rome—and I had a wooden sword, and I still have a scar on my little finger to prove that I fought with it. I basically stood there itching in a black polo-neck sweater while other actors went on with huge speeches. Nobody knew what anybody else was saying, except you knew that when the guy stopped talking it was your turn to start.

THE FOCUS

I worked at the Focus Theatre under Deirdre O'Connell—most young actors worked under Deirdre for various lengths of time. She gave me my start, and she was a fabulous teacher.

She used to say, "Gabriel, there's one thing that you have to learn about working on the stage: it's that the audience shouldn't know when you're going to come on, because if it says in the play that you've gone away to Moscow and you may not return, you want to keep that sense of tension among the audience.'

I said, "What do you mean?"

She said, "Before every entrance that you make, I can hear you in the wings, clearing your throat." I became known in the Focus Theatre as "the Croup." Other actors—and the audience— would know that it was time for me to come on, because they'd hear me in the wings.

THE PROJECT

One day I got a call from somebody who said, "If you're looking to become an actor, you can come to this place called the Project." So I went to the

Project. Everybody was there: Neil Jordan, Liam Neeson, the Sheridans. . . . It was a great time to be a young actor in Dublin.

I left teaching that year, so I was no longer a teacher, I was an actor; and so instead of a tweed sports coat from Clery's, I was now to be seen walking around the streets of Dublin sporting waistcoats and collarless shirts and jeans with high boots, telling people I was an actor.

I never really had any doubts about changing like that. I've always been into change; I've never believed in staying in the same thing for very long, as you can gather. I didn't want to be there at seventy, still doing the same thing—to be an old white-haired teacher in a stained waistcoat, and the kids saying "Oh no, not this eejit again."

1977 Dublin hadn't had the great artistic explosion we know now. We were the first of it. All the actors at the Project couldn't get into the Abbey or the Gate, because they couldn't speak properly, or they hadn't gone to drama school. The Project sprang up to accommodate actors like that. I remember it being one long marijuana-smoking, drinking, Rabelaisian party till seven o'clock in the morning. "What's the next play?" "We're off to Edinburgh!" "We've just won the Fringe Award!" "Where are we going next?" It was an incredible roller-coaster of excitement, of bohemianism, or so it seemed to me—going from the excitement of television studios to rehearsal halls.

I lived in a little apartment on Stamer Street, just off the South Circular Road, which I paid £2.50 a week for. Johnny Murphy, a friend of mine, said it was the only apartment in Dublin where you had to wipe your feet on the way out, it was so dirty inside. And there were seven Nigerian apprentice doctors downstairs, me in the middle with no lock on the door, and upstairs a couple of people who I never saw, though I suspect they were up to nefarious doings in the underworld in Dublin. I ate fish fingers and apples and was never in.

I got my Equity card in a play called *The Liberty Suit*, at the Olympia Theatre, in 1977. I had just been to Tenerife on my holidays and was completely suntanned, and there was no line inserted in the script to explain how my character, a car thief who'd been in jail for four years, had managed to acquire a Mediterranean tan. . . . And then I got my first television job, which was as a curate in a play called *The Last of Summer*. I had to show Susan Fitzgerald into a room in which Barry Casson was playing the bishop, and I knocked over a statue of the Blessed Virgin, smashed it into a thousand pieces. I had no lines, but I caused hundreds of pounds' worth of damage, and endless letters between the Convent of Mercy and RTÉ.

Funnily enough, I think I did some of my best work as an actor in those times. I did comedy, which I love, though people don't really cast me in it now because they think I'm such a dour, brooding kind of guy—which I am and I'm not. I really felt I was an actor, and I was fresh and young and excitable, and ready and open and unspoiled by the sight of anything. I feel I did my best theatre work there.

I don't really miss theatre. I admire great theatre, but to be honest I haven't seen it with any regularity. Also, I feel that the stage as a method of expression is now an actors' medium. It doesn't really speak to a lot of people any more, and it's become elitist, both in terms of the kind of people who go to the theatre and the kind of things that it addresses. And it doesn't really speak to me any more. I rarely find my concerns dealt with in a theatre.

I'd like to do a play now and again, because it is an actors' medium and there are roles there that

The Usual Suspects: (from the left) Kevin Pollak, William Baldwin, Benicio Del Toro, Gabriel and Kevin Spacey.

"I think that the idea of Hollywood is far more potent that the reality of it . . . and that the place that we look for as Hollywood doesn't really exist at all, or only exists somewhere in the mind."

you just can't do on film. But I have no great desire at the moment to do it.

CINEMA

EXCALIBUR

John Boorman came to see *The Liberty Suit*, and he asked me to be in *Excalibur*, which was my first

break. (I had a naked scene in *The Liberty Suit*, and when I met John Boorman's daughter Daisy in England a few years ago, she came over to me and said, "You were the first naked man I ever saw." I was very flattered.) I hoped that I was going to have long, flowing hair and look incredibly romantic, and John Boorman says, "Well, I think we should cut the hair." And my heart sank, and I thought, Oh God.

But I had a great time doing that movie. I was

working with Nicol Williamson—he told me later on that he could never understand anything I was saying. I was on top of a horse, and the armor stuck into the top of my neck, so when I said "The land from here to the sea shall be yours," Nicol Williamson turned to John Boorman and said, "He's saying something about his granny!"

In the atmospheric thriller, Defence of the Realm, *1985.*

I had my first on-screen love scene in that. I didn't know anything about the technicalities of making love on screen; I thought that they came along with a camera and put it down and you did the thing, just like on the stage, and the camera captured all the angles. I didn't understand that you had to do it this way, that way, put the camera here, put the camera there, et cetera, et cetera.

So I was doing the scene with John Boorman's daughter Katrine, who was playing my wife, and I was supposed to make love to her in quite a violent fashion. They did the wide shot, which was me on top of her in my suit of armor, and a fire burning behind me. I was covered in sweat. Anyway, I made love to Katrine in the wide shot, doing my grunting and groaning and all those medieval sexual shenanigans. Then they came in for the close shot and I was there saying, "Are we going to do it again?"

"Yes, we've got to get the close shot."

So then I see them putting a pillow onto the bed, and I hear John Boorman saying, "Okay, Gabriel, can you . . . ?"

I'm saying, "Where's Katrine?"

"Oh no, she's not going to be in this shot."

"So I have to hump the cushion?"

"Yes, yes, yes."

That was the beginning of my disillusionment with it. I don't care how into the part you are, there's always a part of your brain that tells you, "You are making a complete eejit of yourself. Everybody knows that that's a cushion, and besides, you're wearing a suit of armor, and who ever heard of anybody raping anybody in a suit of armor?"

Anyway, I did the scene, and I believe I got a round of applause at the première in Dublin for doing the job with armor on. People used to say to me, "Come 'ere, you were in that movie—how did you do it with the gear on ye?" It was a question I was often asked by learned critics.

BRITISH FILMS

In about 1981 I went to the National Theatre in London, and I began to work in British films. I'm very fond of that period in my career, because I made what I think are some pretty good films. I did a movie called *Defence of the Realm*, which I think was a very forward-looking movie for its time. I'm very proud of that film. And then I did a couple of risky movies—like I worked for Ken Russell. People ask me why. Well, I played Lord Byron for Ken Russell, and I don't know many actors who would've turned down that role. I played a kind of Lord Lucan character in a movie called *Diamond Skulls*, which wasn't entirely successful but I was happy that I had done it.

I look back at those movies now and there was no reason why I should not have done them. They were all leading roles, good directors, very interesting scripts. To have a successful movie is a rarity. It took me a long time to realize that for every successful movie you see, you can count forty that are box-office failures.

AMERICA AND HOLLYWOOD

I went to America because I had a curiosity about it; I was going to go there whether I was in movies or not. And I went there and I found myself being offered a job. And then I got married there, and that tends to keep you in a particular country.

In Britain I felt that the people were—not resentful, but that they didn't quite go out of their way to be hospitable to foreigners; but America was different. America is a country of transients, of immigrants; people have come there from somewhere else. So there's not the same kind of antipathy towards foreigners—outsiders are welcomed. And that makes a profound difference to the way you feel about yourself in a particular country.

I like living in Los Angeles. I like my house there, I like my life, my children are there, I like the sun. I know that's a very prejudiced view of Los Angeles, because I also know the negative side of it. But to me, Hollywood is a pleasant place where I live. It's the center of my business—if you made cars you would live in Detroit. I'm lucky to be able to get home as often as I do.

I don't have any real ambition to do anything. There are no great parts I want to play, I don't feel in competition with anybody. I don't think that anybody gets the roles they expect. There are very, very, very few good roles around. Al Pacino, Robert De Niro, Dustin Hoffman—why do you think they work once a year, sometimes once every two years? Because that's how long it takes for a good role to come their way again.

But to be working in film is a thrill beyond belief, because I never thought that I would be doing that. Whether I do it in Ireland or England or Israel, or wherever, the joy of making movies never really dissipates. And I'm moving out into producing, writing, and so forth, so I feel I'm constantly involved.

Every movie is a gamble. A good script does not necessarily make a great movie—it can be turned into a successful movie, by the right combination of editing and directing and so forth. Anybody who thinks they can plot a career making great movies has to be either extremely privileged or extremely careful in what they do.

Funnily enough, as a child I always preferred British movies, the black and white movies of the fifties. I loved Terry Thomas and Peter Sellers, and all those guys. I guess I felt I could identify more with the English movies because Hollywood to me was such an inaccessible place. There was a part of me that didn't believe it really existed.

I'm still looking for it today. I think that the idea of Hollywood is far more potent than the reality of it, because I think that the inaccessibility of Hollywood when you actually go there further strengthens the idea that it is some kind of a mythical place. And I sometimes think that the place that we look for as Hollywood doesn't really exist at all, or only exists somewhere in the mind.

I think that every art form has its cycle. I think painting, for instance, was much more important centuries ago than it is today, in terms of how it influenced popular perception and perspective. Literature, I think, was more powerful a century ago. Radio has lost a lot of its power. And movies are beginning to lose their power too. Movies had their golden age, in the thirties and forties; the fifties, I think, at least for me, wasn't a great time for movies; then in the sixties you had a kind of rebirth, a renaissance. But now a lot of the movies are what I call McMovies—they're thought up by marketing people for a target audience, and they deal with a very limited range of subjects. And now in Hollywood they're remaking all the movies they made in its golden age. . . . It's like they've come to the end of the road. The monster is eating its own tail now, and it'll eat itself up until it eventually annihilates itself.

LEADING MAN

If you had told me maybe fifteen, sixteen years ago that this was going to be my lot in life, that people were going to say that I was handsome, and a leading man and stuff, how could I have believed it? It's so far removed from any idea I had of myself that to this day I don't think I've ever really sat down, even for two seconds, and basked in the glory of that type of image. The image I have of myself is the only image that's real to me—it may not be what other people see, but it's the only one I think of as real. So if anyone says to me that I'm handsome or a sex symbol, their words have almost no effect whatsoever on me. Yet because people say it a lot, it must have some reality for them. But I've never been able to enjoy it, and it's never done me much good.

I used to be ashamed of my broken nose for a long time, and I thought that if only I had a nose like Cliff Richard, the world would be my oyster. When I was much younger, I didn't like turning sideways. . . . These are the things that affect you when you're sixteen, seventeen. You think you're an abhorrence, because you don't look like what you regard as the ideal.

I used to think, when I went to dances and sat in the corner petrified, that maybe I could turn my petrification into some kind of sexual allure. I was hoping that some girl would say, "God, who's that incredibly interesting guy over there in the corner who doesn't say anything, and just kind of looks at the floor? Maybe he's somebody I could get off with." They never actually said that; they just said, "Jaysus, who's that bore over in the corner? Make sure you don't get caught over there."

FILM IN IRELAND

I think there's a great myth about the Irish film industry. What does it really boil down to? A couple of huge, mega-budget productions that come in every so often—*Braveheart, Far and Away*. These

gabriel byrne

huge-budget movies are an aberration, they're not going to be a consistent factor of life in films in Ireland. Then at the other end of the scale you get a plethora of low-budget movies that come in here—I'm talking specifically from the actor's point of view—where they use actors for less money. It's cheaper to make them here, everybody speaks English, et cetera. It's not really a film industry as such. You can only speak of an "industry" in Hollywood, where there's the infrastructure to support one. And Hollywood's been there for more than sixty years.

What we have at the moment is a pattern, that may or may not even out, of major-budget movies coming in every so often, but mostly low-budget movies being made. A lot of them feature Irish actors only in supporting roles—something which has consistently plagued our business over the years. Yes, it means work for crews, but a lot of these crews are coming in from England and America. There doesn't seem to be any place for young people to go to learn the craft of making a movie. Where do you go in Ireland if you want to learn to be a screen actor, a cameraman, a director, a producer?

A couple of people, like Jordan and Sheridan, have had success abroad. But it's misleading to think that American audiences are just waiting for Irish movies, because they're not. The truth is that no Irish movie apart from *The Crying Game* has been a spectacular success in America. And for a film to be a spectacular success in America, it has to, number one, make money. It's not just enough if it gets critical reviews saying "This is a great movie," or if it is nominated for Oscars. In terms of practical success, a giant sweep-the-boards movie is not happening in Ireland. And even if it does, it's not going to lead to an Irish film industry, because we can't support it here. In practical terms, in

wintertime it's dark at half-past three. That's why people went to Hollywood in the first place—because of the weather and because of the light.

I've tried to work with the Irish film industry in my own way, by coming back here to do movies. I think we've moved away from the literary kind of convention, where we used to write short stories and poetry and so forth; people are now beginning to focus on trying to make movies. And I like working with young writers and young directors and helping them get things off the ground and so forth. To date I've done five movies here, and I think it's important that people who achieve a bit of success abroad come back and put something back into the country. There's absolutely no reason why they should, but I think it's nice if they do.

My roots are still in Ireland, and my Irish background is very important to me. I feel that it's really important that Irish people get to make their own movies, because the perception of Ireland out there comes mostly through American movies. When you ask most Americans who have never been here about the country, they'll think of a movie they've seen and say, "Oh, that's what it's like." So what we get out there is important.

THE ACTOR TURNS PRODUCER

My producing career is opening up in the States, and I'm now a major producer with the studio system in Hollywood. I have just signed a major deal with Columbia for two years. It's very exciting to be able to develop and produce my own material. I won't develop anything I'm not passionate about—I'm not going to waste two years of my life. I ask myself, What is important to me, what do I want to say about my life and the world around me, and can I make a movie about that?

I've made a movie about the tinkers in Ireland—that's *Into the West*, which I stuck with for four and a half years. *Into the West* was really an accident, in that Tim Palmer, with Michael Peirce, was the original creator of the idea. We all just muddled along and tried to make the movie. We didn't really know much about producing, but I learned a lot.

After a while it became a kind of obsession. The movie was about something that was very close to me—the idea of a father trying to communicate with his children, in extremely abject conditions. And it was also about the children looking for a mother, the idea of alienation, and the isolation of the Irish gypsies, the Irish traveling people. And it was about the idea that the line between fantasy and reality is actually very, very thin. There were a lot of themes in this movie. It's had a profound effect, I think, on a lot of the people who've seen it. I think Jim Sheridan wrote a beautiful and profound script.

The next movie was *In the Name of the Father*, which was a book I found and bought, and developed, and then gave to Jim Sheridan. I did the film because I was obsessed with the Guildford Four, the Birmingham Six, the whole British justice system. *In the Name of the Father* was not a very happy experience, and I hope never to have to go through that again. But one of the gratifying things about *In the Name of the Father* is that, despite the falling-out that I had with Sheridan, the movie achieved everything I'd hoped that it would. It gave people an awareness of the plight of those men. It's interesting when people come up to you on the street in America and say, "I never knew about these people." They realize now that the same thing can happen in America—it's not just a British thing. The upcoming movies I'm producing vary from a movie about the nature of romantic love, to a movie about the environment and the culture clash between America and the rest of the world. These are the things that interest me. And I'm going to direct and produce *The Doctor's Wife*, from the novel by my favorite living writer, Brian Moore.

ACTING AND THE ACTOR'S LIFE

Acting, to me, is a mysterious process that I can't even articulate—I believe that in trying to articulate it, it becomes intangible. To me the actor is a channel through which the thoughts and opinions and philosophies of writers pass—he's the vehicle for all that, and he allows himself to be in a state of readiness and preparedness for that.

Acting isn't the be-all and end-all for me. It's important to me, it's how I make my living, but it's not my entire world. In fact, it occupies very little of my world really; I tend to have interests that are altogether outside acting, and I tend to mix with people who are outside acting—although I have many friends who are actors and producers and directors and so forth. But I'm not obsessed by the life of the actor.

I think that the emphasis that's put on the celebrity of the actor, especially today, is misguided. People are obsessed with actors. It has to do with an inherent amazement that someone can adopt the personality of someone else. It's a primitive thing; it's almost like the shaman in a primitive society, who puts on a mask and becomes another character. We're amazed by that. I think film stars occupy the same place in the public imagination as the ancient Greek gods, who had immortality attached to them, once did. We don't like to see our stars get older, we want them to stay the same. And celluloid manages to keep them that way. I remember when Robert Redford's movie *Havana* came out, he was attacked by several critics for looking old. And I remember thinking, How can anybody not remark on how bizarre this is? Do they really, deep down, believe that Robert Redford is not going to age?

Actors being the focus of this attention from the public, which is fed by the media, is disturbing. The new religion now in America is celebrity. Everybody wants to be famous, everybody wants to be a star. And I know a lot of "stars," and I know that being a star is not going to make you happy. If it's something that you crave and obsess about, and desperately desire above anything else, the achieving of it does not bring you contentment. That's a fact. It's not just an easy cliché. There are one or two people I know who celebrity has made benevolent, but in those particular cases it has gone hand in hand with a change of perspective from within.

As soon as you become famous or well-known, a dual reality starts up. Your perception of yourself is one thing, other people's perception of you is another. You're saying, "You're telling me I'm that, I'm telling you I'm this, but you want me to be that, but I have to be this." It's a very dangerous thing. To be honest, *Faust*, about the man who sells his soul to the devil, is one of the very few plays that I really want to do, because basically it's an examination of the bargain you make when you become famous. Whether that fame is thrust upon you or whether you actively seek it out, it brings with it all kinds of problems that nobody can foresee.

So I'm very scared of fame. My life isn't reclusive, but I don't go seeking the limelight, I don't go to premières, I don't go to parties. I don't like being singled out. It's a funny thing: during childhood and adolescence the desire not to be singled out was important; now the desire not to be singled out is still important. That clash between the introspective and the extrovert, which was always

there, still is there.

You kind of get used to celebrity after a while; and then on another level you never get used to it. When I did *Bracken*—the first television series that I ever did in Ireland—I went, almost overnight, from being an unknown theatre actor to being someone almost everyone recognized, and it frightened me. It really did, because I never felt that I had time to get ready for it. It was a bizarre experience, and still is. A television series is an incredibly dangerous thing.

I understand that actors have to work, and they have a job to do—it's just that you have to be very careful how you use your life. And my life outside movies and acting and producing and all the rest of it is very, very important to me. It's more important than acting, it's more important than producing, more important than movies. I don't want to be remembered as a guy who made maybe ten great movies; I want to be remembered by my children as somebody who was a great father, I want to be remembered as a good friend, I want to be remembered as somebody who took chances, who tried to do things that were different. I don't just want to devote my life to being on one movie set after another. And the obsession about fame is so all-encompassing that you can lose sight of who you truly are yourself. I often think, walking down a street: how many people are actually thinking about Clark Gable at this moment? Hardly anyone, I'd say.

I remember Richard Burton—I worked with him just before he died—trying to remember how many movies he'd done. He lost track at about seventy. I said to him, "Why did you make so many movies?" And he turned to me—and I'll never forget what he said: "When I would wake up on a Monday morning, I would say, 'I can't bear reality, I'll do another film'." The film world is a cocoon, it builds a warm shell around everybody in it. Everybody has their function, everybody has a purpose, everybody has a time limit; the world outside ceases to exist, and life is lived in fast-forward for two months. Relationships become intense. It's an unreal world but a very addictive world, and you have to be very careful about becoming addicted to the process of making movies, and to fame. I used to smoke cigarettes—even though I hated them, I still smoked them; and I know people who feel like that about their fame. I'm very wary of the whole thing.

I didn't become an actor to become a Hollywood star, though I hear young actors in Dublin now saying, "Hey, it's Hollywood for me." And there's nothing wrong with having that ambition, but I just wanted to become an actor because I loved being in the theatre, I loved doing plays, I had great fun, great craic. I never dreamed it would be like this. I've been incredibly lucky—but then again, things could just as easily have gone the other way. I often think that sometimes fame is based on an accidental configuration of facial features, and a certain inner vibe, and it's actually got nothing to do with acting at all.

And what people take for acting is sometimes not acting at all. Some people say there are two schools of actors: actors who basically play themselves and allow the work to come through them, actors of the type I hugely admire—like Spencer Tracy, who was always true, always full of integrity, always there in the moment; and then there's the other type of actor, who specializes in false noses and humps, and limps and lisps, and all that stuff. And people think, Wow, that's great acting! But when Olivier was asked to play himself there was nothing there, because he was hiding under his protective shell. It's a kind of acting, all right, but it's spectacular, flashy acting, like the goalkeeper who makes the save with his fingertips, knocking the ball over the bar, and the crowd goes crazy. The other type of goalie is the guy who's on

On location in Ireland for Into the West: *Gabriel with (from left) son Jack, wife Ellen Barkin, and young costars Ruaidhrí Conroy and Ciarán Fitzgerald.*

"My roots are still in Ireland, and my Irish background is very important to me."

ILLUSTRATED INTERVIEWS WITH
gabriel byrne, liam neeson, pierce brosnan, stephen rea, aidan quinn and patrick bergin

the line where he's supposed to be, and when the ball comes, he takes it down without fuss. That's the kind of goalkeeper I admire, and the kind of actor I admire.

I don't know what type of an actor I am. I've never known. I'm sure there are people who hate me as an actor, and there are people who think I'm good. I've long ago ceased to worry about that kind of stuff. When I look back over my career, I don't regard anything that I've done as a mistake. Any mistakes were gigantic learning things for me. And every choice that I've made has been for absolutely the right reason, and has never been based on money or anything like that.

LOVE AND MARRIAGE

My marriage to Ellen Barkin ended recently, but this hasn't disillusioned me about marriage—not at all. I think that longevity, the yardstick by which most marriages—and indeed most relationships—are judged, is fundamentally erroneous. "Oh, so-and-so and so-and-so have been together for forty years, so they have a successful marriage. . . ." I don't see relationships in that way. Various relationships have different time-spans; your allotment with somebody could be two years, it could be twenty years, it could be ten years. You don't enter a relationship just by accident; you're there not just to try and love the other person, but to try and learn something from them. And every relationship you have teaches you about life and about yourself. I don't regard a marriage as having failed simply because it ends. I believe that what happens is that you come to the mutual recognition of the ending of that particular path, and you must have the honesty to say "I want to go somewhere else."

It's possible that I will get married again—put

an ad in the *Irish Messenger*: "Respectable gent, early forties, non-smoker, pioneer, wishes to meet respectable lady, with view to same"!

I'm not concerned about my children being in this situation. I was concerned for a long time, but I've seen the products of so-called "happy marriages," and they haven't been all that happy. There's no guarantee that just because you live with your parents up to the age of eighteen or nineteen or twenty, you're going to be a well-adjusted, well-balanced individual. That's nonsense—if that was the case, the vast majority of people would be well-balanced and normal. And just because your parents are divorced, there's no reason to presuppose that you're going to be an emotionally damaged adult. Yes, divorce is traumatic, there's no getting away from that; but I think if you are honest with children and they know exactly what's going on, and they know that they are loved by both parents, the damage that divorce causes can be minimized. And myself and Ellen have been more than diligent about making sure that the kids are told, each step of the way, in their own language and in their own terms, exactly what is going on. So they're not being lied to, and they know they have two parents who love them.

I think that at a very early age they're beginning to understand that the nature of love is not simply black and white—that just because you marry somebody when you're twenty-four or twenty-five doesn't mean that you have to stay with them for the rest of your life because convention says so. I don't think so, and I'm here to prove it.

LOVE SCENES

Making love on screen is quite different from the real thing, obviously, but for the most part I've been very lucky with the women I've worked with—Kim Basinger, Bridget Fonda, Kathleen Turner, Greta Scacchi, Lena Olin, Julia Ormond, Melanie Griffith, Nastassya Kinski, Winona Ryder, Faye Dunaway, Barbara Hershey. . . . You have to have a rapport with them; they're as scared as you are about it.

I don't do sex scenes any more. I feel I've gone past that kind of thing. I look at any scene and ask, "Is it absolutely necessary?" If not, I get it cut.

Working in such close proximity to beautiful women has been called an occupational hazard; but I think that people who work in offices, staff rooms, boardrooms—anyone who works in close proximity to anyone else—will have the same kind of temptation.

Infidelity is not confined to Hollywood; it's no more prevalent in Hollywood or on movie sets than it is anywhere. I know a great many people in Hollywood who have incredibly successful and happy marriages. Hollywood is held up as an example, in some way, of what we all aspire to, and so it's under microscopic examination. If somebody there breaks up with his wife or whatever, everyone says "Ah, typical Hollywood"; but the guy down the road could have broken up with his wife. People who live in Hollywood have exactly the same problems as everybody else. The truth is that fifty per cent of American children are the product of divorce, and they don't all live in Hollywood. To be honest, Dublin was a great preparation for Hollywood. Dublin can be a very bitchy, back-stabbing, gossipy backwater, far worse than Hollywood.

BEING IRISH

When you leave Ireland and go away somewhere else, you never really belong in Ireland again. It's a peculiar dilemma that everybody who leaves their own country has to deal with at one stage or another. There's the danger of being in limbo—not really belonging in Los Angeles, not really belonging in Dublin. I now regard myself as not belonging anywhere really. My roots are in Ireland, I am Irish, I am very proud of being Irish; I live in America, but I also live in Ireland; and I'm very lucky to be able to do that.

BEING IRISH IN ENGLAND

Although I lived in England, I never really belonged there. I think most Irish people don't belong there. I used to go to Camden Town and Cricklewood and see Irish people who should never have left their native places, desperately trying to recreate some nostalgic Ireland that no longer existed, in these bars called the King George or the Dog and Duck or the King's Head. And I used to wonder what these people were doing there, and what protection they had from prejudice or discrimination. The answer was none. And I realized that what happened to Gerry Conlon and the Guildford Four could happen to any Irish person, or indeed to any repressed minority. And the irony was that the Guildford Four were from the North of Ireland, so I suppose they would be classified as citizens of the United Kingdom.

When I go to England and I'm stopped by a big policeman at the desk at Heathrow—and this happened to me about five years ago—I can't help but rise up in bile against him, because he took my passport, which was stamped from almost every country in the world, and he said to me in that supercilious questioning voice they have, "Are we going on holidays, sir?" I said, "I don't remember asking you to go on holidays with me." I knew as soon as the words were out of my mouth that I'd be pulled aside and taken in. They brought me to a room—and it's a short step from there to being held under the Prevention of Terrorism Act, and I suddenly saw how this could happen. Fortunately this other guy recognized me from some movie that he'd seen.

BEING AN IRISH ACTOR

When I went into American movies I had to play American roles, and I often say to American actors, "If you had to do a different accent every time you got a job, you'd know what it's like." It's a relief now to be able to play the character Irish if I want, play it American if I want.

I'm tired of going through movies playing Germans, Italians, Israelis, Spaniards, French, English. . . . I've played all those nationalities, but I never really played Irish until I acted in the Coen brothers' *Miller's Crossing*. That was a very important movie for me, because it made a difference. I made it in 1989; I'd just gone to America, and it helped me to become known to American audiences. I played a gangster, and I chose to play the part as Irish because that's what I am, I'm Irish. And *Miller's Crossing* became an Irish movie because I came into it; it became uniquely what it is, an Irish-flavored American period gangster movie.

People have complained to me that it was stereotyping for me, an Irishman, to play a drunken writer in *A Dangerous Woman*. This is ridiculous, ridiculous criticism. Just because you're Irish you can't play people who drink? The truth is that this was a character who was in great pain, who was very lonely, and who drank to relieve his loneliness. He was a fully rounded character of depth, he wasn't a stereotype, and anyone who thinks it's a stereotype really doesn't understand the film or the character.

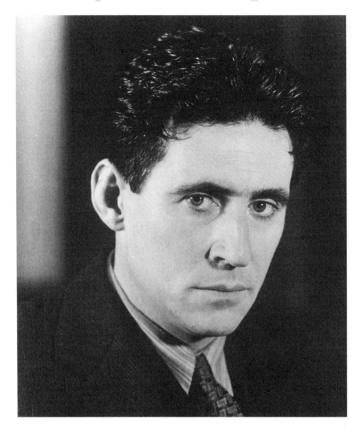

In the Coen brothers' powerful gangster drama, Miller's Crossing.

I don't believe in playing Irish stereotypes—badly written, ill-conceived, generalized stereotypes written usually by people outside this country. Why should I perpetuate that myth by playing these appalling characters? Why should I contribute to that? Hopefully I won't have to do it. To me, it's my choice; but I don't blame other actors who do it, because actors are not supposed to be politicized in any way. That's what Mephisto was about: an actor who could be manipulated by the Nazis to do whatever they wanted him to do. I think that every artistic choice is, in the end, a political act; and that not being politically aware of what's happening in the world about you is naive and dangerous.

ILLUSTRATED INTERVIEWS WITH
gabriel byrne, liam neeson, pierce brosnan,
stephen rea, aidan quinn and patrick bergin

liam neeson

From the penthouse of the Ritz Carlton Hotel in New York, I spotted a rangy figure, jogging with the greatest of ease through Central Park. It was Liam Neeson, on the way to his interview during a break in filming.

IN THEIR OWN WORDS

ILLUSTRATED INTERVIEWS WITH
gabriel byrne, **liam neeson**, pierce brosnan,
stephen rea, aidan quinn and patrick bergin

BEGINNINGS

Liam (second from left), age five, with his sisters Rosaleen, Bernadette and Elizabeth.

I was born in the town of Ballymena, in Wavney Hospital on Cushendall Road, and I think I was eight pounds or something like that. There was a priest who was very good friends with my family, called Liam Mullen—in fact I'm called after him—and apparently he looked at my hands and said "He's going to be a fighter, he's got the hands." Sugar Ray Robinson was World Champion at the time—it was 1952. It was prophetic in one sense, because I took up boxing at an early age.

FAMILY

I have three sisters. We're all stepping stones: one's two years younger, one's two years older, and the eldest is four years older.

I was never spoilt—though I think my sisters would contest that. As regards chores, I was never sent to wash the dishes, but I had to get the coal in and sweep up the yard and stuff like that. It's interesting: now I actually love washing dishes. It's like some people find ironing very therapeutic—I love washing dishes by hand. That's made me very popular sometimes.

I had a classic relationship with my parents—one which was based on empathy rather than on conversation. I think the Irish in general find it hard to talk. My father's deceased now, but communication certainly has improved the older all the rest of us have got, and I think not living together helps, too.

ILLUSTRATED INTERVIEWS WITH
gabriel byrne, **liam neeson**, pierce brosnan,
stephen rea, aidan quinn and patrick bergin

One of the great influences on my life growing up was my grandfather, Jackie Brown. When he retired he used to go to a lot of funerals—he'd walk to them—and invariably he'd be the only man there, just him and the parish priest. Occasionally I'd be dragged out with him, and after the funeral he'd take me into some little country pub; and in my memory there was always a clock ticking, and he seemed to know everybody, or everybody knew him. "Howya Jackie?" "All right"—and that would be the conversation. He would get a bottle of Guinness and I'd get orange juice and a bag of crisps, and I'd watch him sit down and pour the Guinness into a glass; he would turn it about three times, and then lift it up and take a sip, and then there'd be this wonderful exhalation of tension. It was a ceremony he always did. So I aspired to drinking this black, ugly-looking stuff, which is Guinness of course, when I grew up.

My family life was all based on education. I think that's true of most working-class Irish families: there was a great emphasis put on education because it was denied us for so many generations. They knew the importance of finishing your schooling and, if you were lucky enough, going to university to get a degree, which in our parents' and grandparents'

Liam as a teenager.

eyes lifts you out of that rut. I had a great education, wonderful teachers; I also was lucky enough to be an amateur boxer and to be involved in amateur dramatics, so there was never a dull moment.

I must say it certainly wasn't joyous; there was never a lot of money floating around. But there was always food on the table.

MEMORIES

I have a memory of a great-aunt called Sarah, who lived in County Armagh, in a classic Irish thatched cottage with a mud floor. The goats and the hens would come in at night and sleep around the stove. I've asked my mother about that, because I think when I was about a year old I was sent off to Aunt Sarah for nine months—apparently my health wasn't what it should have been, so I was fed on goat's milk and stuff like that. I was a baby, but still I have a memory of that woman in that house, although I've never been back to it. My mother thinks it's a bit weird, but I do remember Sarah. And I remember the Twelfth of July celebrations when I was about three or four—hearing bands for the first time, and big drums. It was pretty terrifying. Ballymena's

ILLUSTRATED INTERVIEWS WITH
gabriel byrne, **liam neeson**, pierce brosnan,
stephen rea, aidan quinn and patrick bergin

predominantly a Protestant community, so the bands were always marching up and down the street, and the spectacle of color and noise was frightening. Even to this day I still get a bad reaction to sound—even a stereo system, if it's turned up to a certain level. It doesn't matter who's playing—I still hate loud music.

My grandfather was a steam-engine driver. His route was from Dublin to Waterford and Waterford to Cork, and I remember—I guess I would've been seven or eight—my mother taking me to the station in Waterford when my grandfather was due in, and seeing this black monster pull into the station, and my grandfather descending through a cloud of steam down these stairs with his hat and his shiny boots—he was very, very proud of the shine on his hat and his boots. It was like God had just come down from the heavens. And I thought, That's what I aspire to: being a man like that who can control this huge black steam engine.

CAREER CHOICES

I wanted to be a priest at one time. I think the reason for it was that I loved the vestments, and I loved the sense of theatre and drama that went with the Mass. I was an altar boy for six or seven years, and loved every second of it—loved the preparation of laying out priests' vestments, and the specific colors for specific events in the Catholic calendar, and the lighting of candles, and incense and stuff. It was beautiful theatre. And I loved the idea of dressing up in black and being respected, and having everybody tip the hat to you, and being this apparently all-knowledgeable figure who resolved people's conflicts and problems. It's great I'm an actor, because I have played a priest, so I can have my cake and eat it.

I think it's just a phase all kids go through, like wanting to be a fireman. Obviously I wanted to be a steam-engine driver, like my grandfather; then I wanted to be a butcher—I had this obsession with meat and sharp knives. On Saturday mornings I had to go to the local butcher, Barr's Butchers in Ballymena, to get the meat. There was sawdust on the floor, and these huge, big tables, and this guy with his ruddy face, and cuts all over his hands, whistling as he cut the carcass under these extraordinary chunks of meat. It was like an art form.

UNIVERSITY

After secondary school, I went to Ballymena Technical College, which offered pre-apprentice courses, diploma courses and electrical engineering. They also did O levels and A levels. I was fairly competent at scientific subjects; I wasn't great but I had an interest in them. The arts weren't touched at all—you could only do English up to O level, it wasn't offered at all at A level. And what you don't have you don't miss. I mean, now I regret not learning French, and not knowing more about English literature.

I went to university for a year when I was nineteen, but it was an abortive year for me. I always had a flaw or a quality in my character which meant I always wanted to please my elders, especially teachers. I loved knowing, say, that I had a boxing tournament that night and that I also had to get mathematics homework done; I loved being able to do it all, and then go and rehearse for plays, just to be able to say, "Well, I did that—I had a boxing tournament, I also got my maths done, and the physics done, and I was able to rehearse for this play." I just got a kick out of it, pleasing elders.

ILLUSTRATED INTERVIEWS WITH
gabriel byrne, **liam neeson**, pierce brosnan,
stephen rea, aidan quinn and patrick bergin

Rob Roy: *Neeson in the leading role of the eighteenth-century
Scottish folk hero.*

So when I went to university, of course,
nobody gave a damn; there was nobody looking
over your shoulder saying "This must be done for
Thursday." And I was at sea; I just couldn't cope
with this apparent freedom. I couldn't discipline
myself; I basically wasn't mature enough. I used to
just sit in my room in the halls of residence
and literally just stare at walls—not a
thought would go between my ears. I didn't
smoke, I didn't drink, I didn't socialize; I just
wandered around like an aimless, lost soul.

This was what was known as an
intermediate year at university: you did this
year and then you picked the subject you
were going to major in, or do your degree in,
and you went on for three more years. I
knew, coming up to the end of that year,
that there was no way, a) that I was going to
pass the examinations, and b) that I wanted
to stay. So I left—well, I was forced to leave: I
just didn't pass the examinations. And I was
faced with the fact that I might have to pay
back the grant I got for that year—four
hundred pounds or something, which was a
fortune. That didn't happen.

I worked at various jobs, but I felt that,
if only to appease my parents, I should finish
some diploma course. I'd heard about this
teacher-training college in Newcastle-upon-
Tyne that offered a pale imitation of an
actors' training course. So I applied to that,
and got accepted. I spent two years there and
failed again, but I met a lot of people like
myself who were fascinated and eager to do
plays and workshops, and we had a couple of
drama teachers who were actually very, very
knowledgeable about Stanislavski and the
modern dramatic theorists. Richard Cooper,
one of the teachers, introduced me to the
world of Chekhov and Shakespeare. There was a
great repertory company in Tyneside at the time,
and I used to go down there and see all the
productions. We did a lot of plays and things
ourselves, and brought them up to the Edinburgh
Festival. . . . Something really kicked in there.

ILLUSTRATED INTERVIEWS WITH
gabriel byrne, **liam neeson**, pierce brosnan,
stephen rea, aidan quinn and patrick bergin

ACTING

INFLUENCES

Career-wise the greatest influence on me was Colin Blakely, God rest him, who passed away about nine years ago. I remember writing to him after I saw him in Dennis Potter's *Son of Man*, which created a furor. In school, the day after it was first shown, I remember the headmaster and one of the teachers asking for a show of hands in Assembly to see who was allowed to watch *Son of Man* last night on television; and we got a bit of a ticking-off because we shouldn't have been watching it, we shouldn't have been watching a play portraying Jesus Christ as a man, as a carpenter. And I thought this was one of the greatest performances I'd ever seen.

I think at that age, one is led to believe that Jesus Christ the Son of God is this beautiful celestial figure with flowing robes and hair and a beard, and these extraordinary eyes, who personifies love and

peace. Watching *Son of Man* consolidated him for me and made me think, Well, this man *lived*—and he lived in this period, and he lived in this really hot sticky climate, surrounded by barren rock; and so he had to be tough. Jesus Christ the man was one of the original rebels.

Liam and actress Natasha Richardson on the eve of their wedding, celebrating with his family.

So it made me think not necessarily about Catholicism, but about rebels and guru-type figures, prophets throughout the centuries, from whatever religion, eastern or western. These men were really tough, hard people who had a message to deliver—it wasn't the Hollywood version of *The Greatest Story Ever Told* with Max von Sydow. I mean, he was a genius actor but he was made to portray Christ as if

ILLUSTRATED INTERVIEWS WITH
gabriel byrne, **liam neeson**, pierce brosnan,
stephen rea, aidan quinn and patrick bergin

people could just walk over him. Nobody listens to people like that. Somebody has to grab you by the neck and tell you something. Certainly in my work, you have to tell the truth, you have to firmly believe it, and if you have something to share with somebody, you have to make them listen to it.

When Zeffirelli did his *Jesus of Nazareth*, I remember hearing an interview with Robert Powell, who was a fine actor too. Robert was asked what preparation he did for playing the part of Christ, and what he said stuck with me. He said, "Well, I watched every film version of the story of the Bible, and all the actors who played Christ, they blinked. I wanted to play Christ where he doesn't blink." And I thought, That's research? Sure enough, if you watch the film, Robert Powell never blinks, and he's got these fantastic eyes. But I just remember thinking, That's the dumbest thing I've ever heard.

Colin Blakely was from Bangor, and he played Christ as a tough little man who had a mission in life. It was a revelation about religion, as well as a revelation about what an actor could actually

The Academy Awards 1994: Best Actor nominee Neeson (for Schindler's List*) with Natasha Richardson.*

achieve, and what a writer could actually achieve.

So I promptly wrote to Colin Blakely and was very surprised and flattered to get a handwritten letter back, which I still have. I told him how I wanted to be an actor, and he told me that when he first went over to London he saw Alec Guinness once in Woolworth's somewhere in London and marched up to him. Guinness told him that he should go to drama school, so Colin was passing on that knowledge.

"Always remember," he said, "you must always, always remember you have to eat." He put that in block letters—YOU HAVE TO EAT—and underlined it. I think he was intimating that you shouldn't just waft into acting thinking it's all going to be great; it's a real hard life. Later, in 1980, I had the chance of doing a two-hander play with him on television, and he remembered me from this letter—which was great, because I was nobody. We struck up a really good friendship, and I loved the man, I really did. I thought he was a truly great man and a wonderful actor. He was a huge influence.

ILLUSTRATED INTERVIEWS WITH
gabriel byrne, liam neeson, pierce brosnan,
stephen rea, aidan quinn and patrick bergin

THE LYRIC

By the time I left the teacher-training college, I was obsessed with being an actor. I didn't know how to go about it—I felt I didn't want to go to RADA [Royal Academy of Dramatic Arts], or somewhere like that, and in fact I wouldn't have got a grant to go anyway.

So I went back home and worked in an architect's office, always bragging to these architects that I was going to be an actor. But as the months passed, it was like, What the hell, how am I going to set this in motion?

And then one of the guys in the office called my bluff. He said, "Well, you should call up to Lyric Players Theatre, in Belfast," which was a repertory company. So I called up, and I was fortunate enough to talk to Mary O'Malley, who was the founder of the theatre. I blurted out to her whatever experience I had as an amateur actor, and how I had done this kind of an actors' course in Newcastle. And the first thing she said to me was, "What height are you?" I said, "I'm six foot four." She said, "Be up here next Thursday, ten o'clock." Then she asked what I was doing, and I said, "Well, I'm at work," and she said, "Can you take the day off?" and I said yes.

So I went up—I took the day off work and didn't tell my parents. I'd prepared a bit of Shakespeare, something from an American play, I think a bit of Yeats, and some other piece I can't remember.

Suddenly I was standing on this stage, and Mary O'Malley was sitting in the audience—it was just me and her. I went through this and I don't think I was terribly good, but I think she saw something raw, or at least a hunger to do this. She gave me this script by Joseph Plunkett, called *The Risen People*— there's a speech Jim Larkin makes, and she said, "Have a look at that and read it," and I read it.

Afterwards I sat down beside her and she said, "Do you really want to be an actor?," and I said "I do." She outlined to me how hard it would be, and told me that there wasn't a great deal of money in it. But I sensed that something was going to happen here. And I went into her office and she offered me this play. I signed a British Actor's Equity contract that day. I could not believe it. And the irony was that I was getting fifty pence more being an actor than I was in this architect's office—I got thirty-one pounds fifty pence.

I went down to York Street train station to get the train back to Ballymena, and there was serious trouble in the streets, but I was jumping over barricades, shaking hands with the soldiers and showing them this contract. I got off the train at home and went to this local hostelry I used to go into, called the Globe Bar—it isn't there any more. And of course the pints of Guinness were consumed at a rate of knots, and I was showing this contract to everybody and anybody, so by the time I got home this contract was like an ancient parchment, it had so many lines and creases on it.

I think my parents were quite shocked, but they realized that this was what I wanted to do and had to do, if only to get it out of my system.

I just wanted to be an actor. I felt the pinnacle would be to play Hamlet in the Royal Shakespeare Company or at the National Theatre. But in the Lyric Theatre, we were doing a play every four or five weeks, and that stops you from forming a plan, because you're just learning lines all the time.

I remember that after the first year I got a severe strain of hepatitis—I don't know what strain it was, but I was basically just run down. I wasn't eating well. So I recuperated from that and it taught me a lesson. As Colin Blakely said, you have to eat, you have to look after yourself.

ILLUSTRATED INTERVIEWS WITH
gabriel byrne, liam neeson, pierce brosnan,
stephen rea, aidan quinn and patrick bergin

DUBLIN

Then I worked in Dublin for two and a half or three years. I moved to Dublin because I felt I'd learned as much as I could in Belfast. I've always had an acute sensitivity to knowing when I'm not growing or learning any more. I'm indebted to Mary O'Malley for the training I got at the Lyric Theatre, and to Roy Heybeard who ran the Arts Theatre at the time. I had been working with these wonderful actors—Louis Rolston, and Bill Hunter, and Stella McCusker, and Trudy Kelly—but there comes a point when you think you're starting to repeat yourself in some way.

We were down in Dublin doing a Joseph Tumelty play at the Eblana for a week, and Peter Sheridan came to see it and left at the interval. He met me afterwards and said, "Jaysus, I hated the play, it was an Ulster farce, that's what it was"—but he was casting for *Says I, Says He*, by Ron Hutchinson. Art Ó Briain was directing, and I met him and read for him, and I got offered this play. I was ecstatic. Dublin just seemed to be made up of Gabriel Byrne, Ronan Wilmot, Bríd Brennan, Mannix Flynn, Peter Caffrey, Garrett Keogh, Paul Bennett—all these great actors. . . . It felt like I was in the right place.

New York City, 1996.

"The only time I really set my mind to trying to achieve something was when I moved from London . . . to go to America. That was a definite drive. I felt I had to go there."

I was in *Says I, Says He;* then we did *Streamers,* an American play about the Vietnam War, by David Rabe, for the Dublin Theatre Festival. Then Ronan Wilmot and I did a little one-act play by Lady Gregory—*Rising of the Moon*, I think it might have been called; I can't remember—for the lunchtime play at Trinity College. *Says I, Says He* went to the Abbey. We did quite a few plays in the Peacock and the Abbey—*Aristocrats* by Brian Friel was one of them. I love Brian Friel's work; as an amateur and a professional I've done five of his plays, and I just love his craftsmanship. As a writer he understands actors, and acting, and the theatrical process. And he gives you characters on a platter.

ILLUSTRATED INTERVIEWS WITH
gabriel byrne, **liam neeson**, pierce brosnan,
stephen rea, aidan quinn and patrick bergin

In one of his finest roles, as the Irish revolutionary and statesman Michael Collins, *directed by Neil Jordan.*

"I think that if we ever sit back and think, This is who I am, and this is what I stand for, and then don't change until the day we die, we will be missing something extraordinary—an extraordinary gift to develop and to change."

It was a really exciting time. At first I had nowhere to live—for two nights I slept in St. Stephen's Green; the rest of the time Peter Caffrey and Mannix Flynn, who shared an apartment, or Christine Sheridan were gracious enough to give me a bed or a couch to sleep on. But at that age, and at that time, you didn't worry about stupid things like where you were going to sleep; you were just consumed by the artistic energy that was in Dublin then.

"EXCALIBUR"

John Boorman came to see a production of *Of Mice and Men*. Ray McAnally, God rest him, had adapted and directed it. John was getting *Excalibur* together, and I remember meeting him over in the Flowing Tide, the pub across from the Abbey, and being very taken with him. I'd always admired Boorman. And after that meeting I went out to Ardmore Studios and saw Camelot being built, and suits of armor

ILLUSTRATED INTERVIEWS WITH
gabriel byrne, **liam neeson**, pierce brosnan,
stephen rea, aidan quinn and patrick bergin

being fashioned, and horses being led around with medieval saddles on; and I thought, Oh, this is something else! John told me that he was going to film the Arthurian legend, the whole story—and for five million dollars. It seemed like a fortune to me, but he made that film on a shoestring. And he wanted to use, bless his cotton socks, as much Irish talent both behind the camera and in front of the camera as he could. He got a lot of resistance from producers, but he was adamant about that.

And then I got offered the part of Sir Gawaine. I remember reading the script; not knowing the process, I read the part that Gabriel eventually played, which was Uther Pendragon, and called up Boorman, saying "Hey, John, any chance I can play Uther Pendragon?"

He said, "Oh, it's been cast."

I said "Oh."

"But with Gawaine," he said, "you'll be in the film the whole way through; Uther's only in it for six weeks." And I thought, Twelve weeks doing a movie—the experience alone will be great.

And it was. The cinema bug definitely got under my skin then. And John was such a wonderful teacher; he's a great editor, that was his training, and he would explain to you why he was setting the camera in this position, what he was going to shoot—he would tell you how much of the scene he would use, and why he was changing the camera angle, and he would invite us behind the lens to see what he was shooting. It was extraordinary how he took the time to do that, and I loved him for it. He was a real influence about the technique of film acting.

AMERICA

I never really set out to plan or forge a career. I was always aware that eighty or eighty-five per cent of actors are always out of work, in this country as well as back home. And I always felt, and still do feel, very fortunate when I get offered a piece of work, and I hope that never changes.

The only time I really set my mind to trying to achieve something was when I moved from London—I lived in London for seven or eight years—to go to America. That was a definite drive. I felt I had to go there. In London I was fortunate because a lot of American mini-series were always being made there and I was cast in them; but then the English pound got very strong against the dollar, so those companies weren't coming in any more. Months of unemployment were looming ahead. I remember I had a little flat in Stockwell, and I was sitting there one afternoon, one of those London days when it gets dark at about one in the afternoon, and I thought, To hell with this. I'm going to do something.

So I went down and saw my bank manager, saw how much I had in the bank, and withdrew it. I was on my own, and I felt, Well, I'm just going to go out and see what happens. I had made a rough tentative arrangement with two agents out in America—I had done a recce a year before, when I'd gone out with my then English agent Norman Boyak and met some of these agents; and these two guys, Scott Harris and Howard Goldberg, were the only agents who actually listened, who were interested in me. The other ones were all saying, "Well, you're too big, you talk funny, I don't think we can do anything for you." But these two guys were young, and they were hungry and keen, but they said there was nothing they could do for me while I was in England. So having made this decision, I called them up and said, "Look, can I come out in . . . ?"—I think it was December or January. "I can live for five or six weeks, and I do not want to sit in a hotel room, so it's up to you guys. I'll meet anybody and everybody."

And that's what I did. They sent me out on casting calls, and those went on forever—for parts of Red Indians, you name it. . . . All I asked of them was not to say I was an Irish actor. They could say I was an actor from Ireland, which is different, or that I was European. So within the six weeks I managed to get the part of an American serial killer in one of these movies of the week. It paid thirty thousand dollars, which was a fortune. It meant I could stay on in this little grungy hotel for at least a bit longer. And then work breeds work, and I slowly discovered that Hollywood is actually a village, and if you're a new face in town and you equip yourself well, people get wind of it.

I was just fortunate. I went from job to job to job, and I was always packing a suitcase and heading off somewhere. I didn't give a damn if I was tenth choice, if nine other actors had turned down the part. It didn't matter. It was just an amazing experience, acting in front of a camera. And then the point came when I thought, Why do I still have this little apartment in Stockwell in London? So I sold that and officially made the move to live here and applied for a Green Card and all that. And I never looked back once.

MOVIES

"MUTINY ON THE BOUNTY"

I played the Richard Harris part in the remake of *Mutiny on the Bounty*, about ten years ago. That was exciting because it was the one big film that was being cast in London, and every actor, every actor, was going up for some part in it. I got cast because I was twenty or twenty-five pounds heavier than I am now, and I certainly looked like a thug, which is

exactly what I think the director, Roger Donaldson, wanted. And the prospect of going to Tahiti! I thought, I can live with that, only to find when we got there that we were actually on this island called Moorea, which is a ten-minute flight from Tahiti itself.

It was beautiful, Paradise on earth, for the first two weeks. After two weeks . . . There's a name for it; it's the opposite of cabin fever. It's when you're surrounded by water and the nearest land mass is thousands of miles away, and it's actually what happened to the real mutineers. We would all turn on each other over the tiniest things—like if someone borrowed an English newspaper, be it the *Sun* or the *Daily Mirror,* and it wasn't given back the next day, even if you had read it cover to cover, it would be very near fisticuffs. That's what happened to the original mutineers. They all came from the slums of England to Paradise, and the Tahitian men and women were extremely gracious and giving. . . . These poor guys, in the eighteenth century, must have thought they were in heaven. I would have mutinied.

"THE MISSION"

The Mission was shot in Colombia and Argentina. That was really interesting, because again, I had a small part in it but I was there for nearly the whole shoot. And it was interesting to watch three different schools of acting, so to speak. There was Robert De Niro, who to many people personified the Method school of acting; there was Ray McAnally, whom I knew very well—he'd directed me and I'd acted with him on stage—and who had his own attitude to it, I think; and then there was Jeremy Irons and a whole group of other really good English actors. It was a chance to see them out of their milieu, literally in the middle of a jungle, and

ILLUSTRATED INTERVIEWS WITH
gabriel byrne, **liam neeson**, pierce brosnan,
stephen rea, aidan quinn and patrick bergin

to watch their processes at work.

And on top of that we had three hundred Colombian Indians, who had no drama in their culture—they don't enact stuff, they don't have ceremonies. They had to be taught what acting was. And as a result, when they did act it was brilliant, because it was all so natural to them that they felt everything. The only trouble was that then they all became directors—they'd all direct each other, and give each other acting instructions. But they were amazing in the most complex psychological scenes and processes, especially in the relationship to the De Niro character. They really were quite extraordinary.

"SUSPECT"

Suspect was one of my first big breaks. It came about because I was actually in Los Angeles. If I'd been living in London or Ireland, there's no way the studio would've flown me over to meet the head of the studio or whatever. And it came about also because I had worked with Peter Yates on a film in London, and Peter was the director of *Suspect*. The studio, of course, wanted a star name; but having got Cher and Dennis Quaid, I think they were happy to go with the director's choice, whether he was a star or not. So I was in L.A. at the time and Peter called me up and said, "Look, go over to TriStar and meet this vice-president of the studio. He just wants to see you, because you're my choice for this part." So I went all the way to Century City, went up forty flights on an elevator, went into this guy's office, and he said, "Oh, so you're the guy Peter Yates is talking about—well, good." And that was the end of the meeting. I got the part; and Peter said, "That wouldn't have happened if you hadn't been in Los Angeles."

It was interesting, acting-wise; because there were no lines to say [Neeson played a deaf-mute homeless man accused of murder], you had to rely on a relationship with the camera, and the editor. I was trying to do little subtle things that sometimes didn't work—sometimes they did, though. In a thriller like that, you have to kind of tease the audience. Peter would always remind me, "No, no, leave an ambiguous feel for the audience: did he kill this person or not? If you show innocence too early, we've no story."

"HUSBANDS AND WIVES"

Husbands and Wives was great. It was great to work with Woody Allen, and I personally thought it was terrific to be in a Woody Allen film. He was very different from anyone I'd ever seen before. He was very, very shy, and very, very quiet, but extremely focused on his work. The film was critically acclaimed, but I didn't think that it was going to make me a star or anything like that. I just felt that it was a recognition that I am a very competent actor; Woody Allen doesn't fart around with the casting of his films.

I know the whole scandal around Woody Allen developed after that, and I think it did affect the film, though not so much in Europe—the French absolutely adore Woody Allen, it wouldn't matter to them if he beheaded people, they'd still go in flocks to his movies. But in the States I think there are people, and certainly people I know of in the industry, who said they would never go and see another Woody Allen movie because of the whole court case with Mia Farrow and the child.

"NELL" AND A NEW PASSION

While I was doing *Nell,* I discovered a passion for fly fishing. I had a Sunday off and I remember going out with two or three teamsters onto this extraordinary lake in the middle of North Carolina, in the Smoky Mountains. For five hours—and for three of those hours it poured with rain—I caught nothing, but I came back transformed. I thought,

I've found my niche in life now. So now I've got all these rods and all these books on fly fishing and flies; and I know it's going to become an obsession. I just know it.

"I don't think that on a deep-down level I have changed at all since I was a boy. . . . I'm still the guy from Ballymena."

FAVORITES

I liked *Excalibur* very much. It really has become a kind of a cult film. I know my technique is nonexistent, but there's a kind of rawness there, even though it's not a huge part; it had a bold and devil-may-care attitude—in fact all the Irish acting is kind of raw and innocent, and beautiful to look at now. I'm very proud of that.

And I'm proud of a film called *The Big Man* that was shot in Scotland five years ago. David Leland directed it. I loved working on that film, and I was astounded at the critical reaction it got from the English press. One reviewer from one of the top-notch papers in England said that the only place where this film should find an audience was Bulgaria or some communist-bloc country like that. Of course the film was set in the

ILLUSTRATED INTERVIEWS WITH
gabriel byrne, **liam neeson**, pierce brosnan,
stephen rea, aidan quinn and patrick bergin

aftermath of the coal-miners' strike; and the hardship that my character has to go through, and what he resorts to doing to put bread on the table for his wife and kids, is harrowing. It got a really violent reaction from the English press, but I think it's a really good film. It's not like a little BBC drama about a guy living in Scotland; it has universal epic proportions.

What else? I'm very fond of *Darkman* because I always love those classic fifties films—*Jekyll and Hyde, The Invisible Man, Wolfman,* and all those B horror films—and *Darkman* was a kind of a homage to all that, and it was also slightly tongue-in-cheek. And it was a chance to wear unbelievable amounts of prosthetic make-up. I took this as a challenge—it was like Greek tragedy, where you wear a mask and have to present a personality through it. I didn't realize it would be a nineteen-week shoot, with five hours of make-up every morning. It was really tough, but it's a great escapist film. It's interesting—here in New York, all the black brothers love that movie: "Yo, *Darkman*, give me five!' So I'm kind of protected by the black community, and since *Schindler's List* I'm kosher with the Jewish community.

REGRETS

There's no film that I would want to buy all the prints of. There are a couple I haven't seen, because I had a miserable time doing them, and I have no interest in seeing them. But even the worst weren't bad—there's always something to learn, there's always someone you'll befriend and work with again. There's never a really bad experience. I've made about twenty-six films, and maybe there are a couple of people I would choose not to speak to again, or who I certainly don't send Christmas cards to, but that's not bad after so many films.

There are some movies that I did to pay the rent. I was fortunate enough to be asked to do them and I thought, Yes, I can do this, knowing full well that it would score a zero at the box office and a zero with the critics. But as Colin Blakely said, you have to eat. If you don't work, the bills still come in.

LIFESTYLE

LIVING IN L.A.

I live in New York now because I lived in L.A. for seven years, and I found it a very strange lifestyle. It was all-consuming, and it was all about movies and the movie industry, and it had a weird effect. It almost turned me right off, even off the process of acting. You're surrounded by these huge buildings, all edifices to the fact that the movie industry is an industry and can make billions of dollars, and I was fast losing touch with why I wanted to be an actor in the first place. It was all about getting parts, and the politics of parts, and the politics of this studio or that studio, and I just found I was getting lost. I found my level of cynicism went up three hundred per cent, to the point where I was being detrimental to myself. If I got a call to go in and read for a part, I'd think, Well, what's the point? I'm not going to get it, they'll give it to Richard Gere or Jeff Bridges or somebody. . . .

I was working a lot and I bought this little house, and I was certainly very comfortable, but I felt my soul was getting eaten up by myself. I couldn't watch movies, because I couldn't escape into the movie theatre—I don't mean I was recognized, not that at all, but I was watching films with a professional eye, looking at the camera moves and performances and stuff. It was as if there was no escape.

NEW YORK AND "ANNA CHRISTIE"

Then I came back here to do *Anna Christie* on Broadway, and that just rejuvenated me. My love affair with New York had actually started two years prior to that, when I did Woody Allen's film *Husbands and Wives* here and bought a little apartment in New York; but this time that love affair was aided by the fact that we were in a hugely successful production—New Yorkers love success and successful people. It was great to get back on stage again, in a part that I feel, without bragging, I was tailor-made for; and it was just amazing that the power of a play that was written seventy-three years ago could touch people. It was wonderful.

In Schindler's List, *his superb portrayal of Oskar Schindler, who saved hundreds of Jewish lives in WWII, earned him an oscar nomination.*

And that confidence it restored in me was perfect for going into *Schindler's List*, because that was all I wanted to bring to Schindler. My preparation time was very, very limited—I had a day—and I thought that if I could come with Schindler's supreme confidence, I could pick up all the rest, or I could do research when I was there.

If *Anna Christie* hadn't come up, I might have left the business. The Lord works in mysterious ways. I'll never forget the first rehearsal for *Anna Christie*. Sometimes in your life there's a feeling that you are somewhere for a specific reason, you're destined to be there, and it's absolutely right. Irrespective of the success of the play, when I was in that room with Natasha Richardson, and David Leveaux, who directed it, and all the other cast members . . . it felt as if I had come home, and Hollywood had just disappeared. Schindler had disappeared. I really didn't care at that stage; I'd done a screen test for Spielberg, but I just thought, Fuck it, this is where I belong. It's a Zen philosophy: if you go chasing after something it's always ahead of you, you never get it; but when you turn your back on it, suddenly it comes up and smacks you on the face. The same thing happened to Tony Hopkins. He went out to Hollywood and chased stardom for nine years, and when he decided to say, "The hell with it, I'm going to go back and do my King Lear," suddenly Hollywood came chasing. It's interesting.

ADVICE

If my eighteen-year-old self were to come up to me and say "I want to be an actor; tell me what to do," I know there's a side of me that would say, just as all our parents do, "Finish your education." But I certainly wouldn't want to turn him off it. I would pass on the advice that Colin Blakely and other

ILLUSTRATED INTERVIEWS WITH
gabriel byrne, **liam neeson**, pierce brosnan,
stephen rea, aidan quinn and patrick bergin

people like Mary O'Malley gave me: realize you're getting yourself into an industry where eighty-five per cent of people are always out of work. Get yourself on the stage; do theatre. Don't think you're going to be a star and walk straight into a television soap. Some people do; but to learn the discipline of acting, what it's all about, you have to do it on stage. That's the advice I have given people.

NORTHERN IRELAND

When I was growing up, I felt I was Irish. My mother was born and reared in Waterford in the Republic of Ireland; my father was from a farming community in County Armagh and had very quiet but heartfelt nationalistic tendencies. He was a very quiet man, so he never totally shared them; but occasionally, if some pompous English politician was spewing forth on the television about Northern Ireland, I'd hear my father going "Grrrr . . . bastard . . . "—you'd hear some grumblings. But I certainly felt Irish, and proud of it.

I actually think there's a bit of Scottish in there too, from the Plantation period; and given my height and profile, and my mother coming from Waterford, I think there might have been a bit of Viking rape and pillage in our family. I've definitely got a Nordic sort of forehead. Certainly here and in Europe people have asked me what part of Sweden or Norway I was from. We've been invaded so many times we're all mongrels. I think we've got a great genetic pool—bits of German, Slav, it's all in there.

I honestly don't know how being Irish has affected me as regards my profession, other than that I feel at ease showing emotion on screen—be it anger or sympathy, or having to cry. But I am Irish, I'm from that stock, and I think it must have effects.

I think I realized there were two communities in Northern Ireland when I was about nine or ten, not because there was any trouble—I grew up in a very, very trouble-free atmosphere—but because in certain years my parents would keep us indoors on the Twelfth of July. I couldn't figure that out, because all my mates were out dancing in the streets and I wanted to go out and join them. So it was then that I sensed a "them and us" attitude.

I'm not sure how that affected me. At an early age I joined the All Saints Boxing Club, which was run and organized by this brilliant man called Father Darragh, who was the parish priest in the town. We were always boxing in tournaments in Belfast against Protestant clubs and Catholic clubs, so it never became an issue. We were always in each other's company, and if there was aggression it was released in the discipline of the boxing ring.

I didn't quite understand the grassroots level of the civil rights marches. I was aware of something monumental going on, but I just didn't comprehend it, even though I was fifteen or sixteen. It came to a head when I went to Queens University for that one abortive year, when I was nineteen. I remember coming back from a physics lecture up the Malone Road in Belfast and wondering why the university was absolutely desolate—there were three students at this lecture, I remember. When I got to the halls of residence a hundred students—I don't know where they came from—all surrounded me, shouting "Scab, scab." Bloody Sunday had just happened—this was a Monday and it had just happened on Sunday. Thirteen people were shot dead, murdered, in Derry. I just remember the embarrassment of being surrounded by a number of people all showing this absolute venom, and also being embarrassed by my own ignorance.

ILLUSTRATED INTERVIEWS WITH
gabriel byrne, **liam neeson**, pierce brosnan,
stephen rea, aidan quinn and patrick bergin

That event galvanized me, in some weird way. From that day on I got into Irish history. I threw physics and mathematics to the wind, and spent as much time as I could in libraries, just learning about my own country, and about the civil rights issues the movement had emanated from.

In school, that knowledge hadn't really been accessible to me at all. My school, St. Patrick's Secondary School, was and still is a wonderful school; but in the history classes we learned about the Great Plague and all those important English dates, and how some dickhead got an arrow through his eye in 1055 or whenever it was—the usual stuff. But Irish history? No, because we were using set English texts for the British curriculum. Irish history, such as the Rising in 1916, got maybe half a paragraph.

I would love to see peace in Northern Ireland. I think people on both sides of the community, Protestant and Catholic, have had enough. They're sick, sore and tired of it. I think there's always been a policy in Britain of divide and conquer. The Protestants and Catholics have so much in common—bad housing, lack of jobs, and stuff like that—and yet they're always kept at loggerheads, which suits certain establishment figures who rule our country.

I have a feeling peace is going to happen in our lifetime. Various talks seem to be going on, officially and unofficially, and I think something is going to come out of them. But it can only happen with full participation from everybody involved—Protestants and Catholics, the Republic of Ireland and Britain. If the Jewish people and the Palestinians can do it—OK, they still have lines to draw as regards the pact they've made with each other—but if they can do it, when their argument goes back thousands of years, we can certainly do it. We can never lose hope. We just can't.

MEN AND WOMEN

Oddly enough, my American male peers seem to have greater difficulty showing their female side. It's interesting: especially after *Schindler's List*, men would come up to me and whisper "You made me cry," as if that was the ultimate. And I'm like, "So what?" They seemed embarrassed about their female side, even though they wanted to share it too.

Leaving aside the Native Americans, after all, America is still only two hundred years old. It's still a young country, and it was forged and won by hard, strong men and women—your classic pioneers, people like Davy Crockett and Daniel Boone, who were originally from Scotland. These are the American folk heroes: they went out and blazed trails through the wilderness, and blazed them through silence, because they had nobody to talk to, they had nobody to share their feelings with. I think the American male character has a staunch kind of stoicism, and it's not seen as manly to show emotions other than anger. That's a sweeping generalization, but I think that the Irish have been brought up in a culture where the storytelling tradition is still very, very strong, and where there's still a belief in the afterlife—be it a fairytale afterlife or whatever—and where the gods and goddesses that we were brought up with were all dominated by women. I think that's infused all our natures, whether we're conscious of it or not. It's a pool that artists, whether musicians or actors or painters, can tap into with a certain amount of ease.

I think it's interesting, too, that books by Robert Bly and Sam Keane are on the bestseller list. In these books, Keane and Bly are basically defining what a man is, what a man should be. *Fire in the Belly* is the Sam Keane book; it argues that men have been confused by the women's movement and the incredible headway that women have made in the

ILLUSTRATED INTERVIEWS WITH
gabriel byrne, **liam neeson**, pierce brosnan,
stephen rea, aidan quinn and patrick bergin

Neeson in the role of Michael Collins, *with Julia Roberts as Kitty Kiernan, and Aidan Quinn as Harry Boland.*

past thirty years, because men weren't a part of that revolution, and they should have been. Bly has this extraordinary theory that ever since the Industrial Revolution, when men had to get up at four or five o'clock in the morning to go to work at the pit-face or in the factory, then come back exhausted, eat their tea, fall asleep in front of the fire and then go to bed, there has been no dialogue between father and son, and that this has led to an absolute alienation of men.

Bly has introduced these courses in America now where men go through an initiation rite—they put on antlers and dance around a fire and share their emotions. They all end up crying and hugging each other and stuff, but they do go through a very, very interesting catharsis. Bly based that on the cultures of primitive tribes all over the world. In some African tribes a boy reaches adulthood at the age of twelve; he's brought out by the elders into the wilderness, and he has to kill a beast, a lion or a bear or whatever it is, and that child comes back a man. Thereafter, even though he's twelve or thirteen, he's treated as a man, and has to respond as a man. Bly reckons that initiation is missing from

Neeson in Schindler's List *with Director Steven Speilberg.*

"'we're looking for peace and happiness. . . . ' And of course that's very important; but to go after happiness, I need to embrace all of life. "

our society. And though I don't agree with everything he says, I think there's a lot of truth to that.

I think a man should be a counterpart of a woman, I think he should reflect a woman. I think he has to have a sense of responsibility for himself, for his family, for the community; he has to have a sense of responsibility for his own feelings. I think all men should be made to wear dresses from the age of fifteen on, for a year. I do, I think they should!

I think that men should be proud of whatever feelings they have, and not be afraid to show them, and always be on a quest to discover what makes a woman tick and what makes them tick. There's

ILLUSTRATED INTERVIEWS WITH
gabriel byrne, **liam neeson**, pierce brosnan,
stephen rea, aidan quinn and patrick bergin

another book on the bestseller list—*Men are from Mars, Women are from Venus*, written by a guy called John Gray, Ph.D. He gives a very simplified psychiatrist's version of the trouble with the sexes: we don't actually accept the fact that we are equal and opposite, that women and men are totally different. And *vive la différence*.

RELATIONSHIPS

I used to say that I was really comfortable with women's company, but I think I'm probably terrified of them. When you live in a very small house, like we did, space is the reason why you fight—if anybody comes into your sphere you'll do anything to protect it. I am very comfortable in women's company and would seek that company out much more than men's—but after a while I have to get away from them, too.

I think that my relationships are predominantly with actresses because they're the people I meet. I would love to have met female bricklayers, and female electricians, but living in Los Angeles, that was extremely difficult.

In a woman, I look for character, very definitely, and beauty is a huge plus. I've always been attracted to physical beauty and talent. And sure could you blame me?

I love women, every shape, size, color, creed. I really do. I think generally speaking they're much better than men in every department, physically as well as psychologically. They get their act together at a much younger age. Men don't, I think, have a real sense of who they are emotionally until their late thirties; women seem to click into that by their late twenties. I admire that. We have to wait a few years to really learn from them.

SELF-KNOWLEDGE

I think that certainly over the past few years I'm discovering more things about myself—some that I'm not particularly proud of, other things where I think, Oh, that's an attribute I didn't know I had. But I think it has to be a constant quest. I think that if we ever sit back and think, This is who I am, and this is what I stand for, and then don't change until the day we die, we will be missing something extraordinary—an extraordinary gift to develop and to change.

I don't know what I'm looking for. I just don't know. I could come out with the glib answers—you know, "we're looking for peace and happiness. . . . " And of course that's very important; but to go after happiness, I need to embrace all of life. You have to embrace pain, and you have to embrace death. And I think maybe that's our quest in life, not to cut out one thing and go after another. To live life is to live life to its full, and that means accepting death, accepting illness, accepting the death of loved ones, disease, bigotry and all the rest of it. You can't shut that out. I guess what I'm looking for is an acceptance of all that. Tolerance.

I don't think that on a deep-down level I have changed at all since I was a boy. Obviously I've developed a bit, just through the sheer fact of being on the planet for as long as I have. I've travelled quite a bit, and I've met a lot of people, and I'd like to think that I've learnt from them—not just people in the industry, but men and women who have touched me in some way. You'd like to think that you've become a distillation of all the qualities these people have. But I think that in the core of myself I haven't changed. I'm still the guy from Ballymena.

aidan quinn

aidan quinn

*While Aidan Quinn was in the middle of
filming in L.A., his publicist, with the best
intentions, arranged the interview in a
Hollywood "Irish" pub. To the dismay of all
concerned, including Aidan, the entire
establishment was covered in stage Oirishry
of every description, from shamrocks to
leprechauns and back—and, to add insult
to injury, was dominated bizarrely by a
huge portrait of the Queen of England!*

IN THEIR OWN WORDS

BEGINNINGS

I was born in Chicago, where my parents had emigrated from Ireland. They went, I think, for the same reasons that most Irish people go—for opportunities, work—all those dreams.

We moved back to Ireland for a year or so when I was about three and a half. Actually, my mother went back with all of us children—at the time there were four of us—because my father was having a hard time getting work, so it was thought that she should go home and stay with her relatives.

FIRST MEMORIES

My earliest memories in life are of being on a farm in Birr, Co. Offaly, and going to a little pre-school, which I did when I was about four.

I remember being asked by the Brother in school to say the prayers at the beginning of the day. For some reason I would not say the prayers, and he was getting mad at me, and he had a cane. My older brother was in the same class, and he kept saying "Say the prayer along with us," and I said, "No, I won't, I won't do it." I remember so vividly the Brother yelling at Declan, "Get Aidan to say his prayers," and Declan saying, "Would you say the

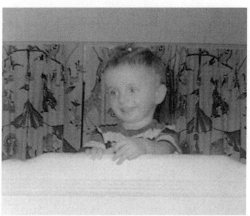

Aidan Quinn (top photo, front) with older brother Declan, who now works in movies as a cinematographer and cameraman.

prayers, for God's sake! What's wrong with you?" And I said, "I won't, I won't say the fucking prayers." And I got whacked repeatedly. I got into some serious trouble when I went home that day.

An aunt of mine told me, when I was doing *The Playboys* a couple of years ago, that she remembers very distinctly me and my brothers and cousins sitting around eating, when I was about three and a half or four; and I rapped on the table very loudly to get everyone's attention, and I said— and she remembers it to this day—"When I grow up, I'm going to be a film star, and I'm going to take care of my mammy."

I was absolutely floored when she told me that. Somehow at three and a half I saw being a film star as the way to go. . . . It's flabbergasting. I don't think there was a local

ILLUSTRATED INTERVIEWS WITH
gabriel byrne, liam neeson, pierce brosnan,
stephen rea, **aidan quinn** and patrick bergin

cinema in Birr, and nobody really had television; I don't think any of my relatives had televisions then. So I don't know where I got it from.

CHICAGO

We kind of went from relative to relative until my father got more on his feet work-wise. He was a teacher by trade, but at the time he was doing whatever he could get. He was an elevator operator, I think he worked in a bookstore, I think he had a few days on a building site . . . anything he could get. I think he finally landed a job at Loyola University—not teaching, but working somewhere. And he brought us all back out.

My parents were like a lot of immigrants: we were completely surrounded by Irish immigrant families, and all my parents' best friends were immigrants. So there was this huge Irish community, almost exclusively Irish immigrants, that we spent most of our time in. I remember a lot of the get-togethers— the parties that our parents would have, where the laughing and singing and dancing went on till the wee hours. There was always laughter. . . .

I also remember difficult things. I remember that when I was about five, me and my older brother were mugged by some weird child-molester-type guy, in an alley right at the back of our house—it was a fairly tough, working-class neighborhood. It was

only just after dark, about five or six o'clock in the evening—not even late. This guy tied our skates together—he was a real weirdo, he was well known in the neighborhood for it—and he punched us both in the face. One of us was bleeding. Then he pulled out a knife because I was crying so much.

The unfortunate thing for the mugger was that he stopped right outside our apartment. I yelled "Mom" as loud as I could, and my mother heard us and came running down the back steps with a broom. My memory of it—and it's hard to tell if it's

With his parents and brother in Chicago, 1961 (Aidan is at right).

"I was born in Chicago, where my parents had emigrated from Ireland. They went, I think, for the same reasons that most Irish people go—for opportunities, work—all those dreams."

ILLUSTRATED INTERVIEWS WITH
gabriel byrne, liam neeson, pierce brosnan,
stephen rea, **aidan quinn** and patrick bergin

real, because these things get repeated—is of her chasing him for half a block, swinging the broom at his head. I think she connected. And we were like, "Get him!"

Then my brother Declan, who's a year and a half older than me, got to ride around with the cops in the Studebaker, looking for him. That was the most disappointing part of the whole incident: they wouldn't let me because they said I was too young. I was really pissed off at that.

With his sister and brothers. Youngest to oldest (left to right): Marian, Robert, Paul, Aidan and Declan.

FAMILY

My mother was always a great storyteller, and my father is a literature professor. So there was always a great love of stories in our household.

I have three brothers and one sister. I have an older brother who's a great cinematographer, a younger brother who's a terrific director and actor, and my sister is a great actress. And I have one wonderful brother who's not in the business, as we call it in California, at all.

I think that Ireland probably has more natural actors than anywhere else I know. It's something that you learn for survival, maybe, very early on. So I guess that might be why so many of us are in the business.

IRELAND

We moved back to Ireland when I was thirteen. We lived in Offaly— Birr—for the summer; then we moved to Dublin.

Coming from the States was a bit of a shock. It was very different. For me that year was a great awakening. We'd moved out of Chicago and into this very WASP community in a smaller city; I was very aware that some people were popular and some weren't, and I was in the "these people aren't" group. But almost the minute we got off the plane and arrived in Birr, I discovered girls, and they discovered me. It was the first time

ILLUSTRATED INTERVIEWS WITH
gabriel byrne, liam neeson, pierce brosnan,
stephen rea, **aidan quinn** and patrick bergin

in my life that girls were interested in me, so I was in heaven.

The place to go courting was Sandymount. The Ormond Tennis Club was there, and there was a beautiful walkway along the river Brosna. We would all walk out that way and go to Sandymount, which is an area of fields just outside of town. There's a public right of way through these lands, and everyone used to go swimming there in the summer. We spent a lot of time there—it was where you went to get away from the town and the windows with everyone staring out, every minute of the day. You got to do your gallivanting and your courting, and all that stuff, out there.

That whole year was a great big holiday for me. I felt that people liked me for who I was— maybe because I was the outsider, the new kid in town. It was a little confusing: by the end of the summer I had pretty much mastered the culchie accent—I didn't want to stand out by being an American—and then we moved to Dublin and I was called "culchie," and some people would get me mad and say "No, he's an American." They didn't know what I was, and I didn't know what I was, so I had to get a Dublin accent to stop standing out. I think when you're that age your voice is much more adaptable, for survival.

I went to St. Joseph's College, in Blackrock. We went home for lunch, which was great. We had an hour and forty minutes for lunch, and my mother would cook us Hafners sausages—these spicy, big, fat, juicy, lovely sausages. . . . God, we couldn't wait to get home for lunch, because we had those every day. There was nothing like that in America; lunch there was half an hour, forty minutes, and that was about it.

I had a good time there; we were always getting in trouble, but that was part of the good time. I had a couple of great teachers—one was a Brother, and one was a lay teacher. And I loved Irish history, I was fascinated by it, so I actually did very well at that, and at English Lit.

But we were cruel—kids are cruel. I remember we had substitute teachers we would just torment— I mean, I think we drove one guy to the loony bin. This guy got hit with more spitballs on the back of the head when he was writing on the blackboard. . . . He'd turn around and get all mad, and we'd all be laughing. When I think of it now—it was terrible, we were terrible.

I did some sports—I was always a sports freak. I had been very into the American sports when I was a kid in the States. I played basketball at Blackrock, and naturally I was very good at it, because I had played it a lot longer than most of the Irish kids. In fact, I believe our team went to the Leinster finals. I remember there was one all-star game I was sent to—I had to get on a bus and go out by Crumlin, I had to change buses twice, and I thought it was a huge journey. I also did long-distance running and track running—until the cigarettes took over and I stopped all of that. Ireland introduced me to the cursed things, and I haven't been able to get rid of them since.

After school in Dublin, me and my friend Larry Byrne used to hang out with two winos who lived in an overturned milk van, right across the street from Dunnes Stores, in a vacant field. There were actually three of them—one came in and out— and we used to hang out with them continually. We'd listen to their stories, and they'd tell us about life, and why we shouldn't be getting into trouble. . . . And they'd also share a little wine with us. We did a lot of that. . . . I guess we were borderline skinheads, bootboys, you know.

I also spent a lot of time in Birr—we'd go down there for weekends. I used to go on my own a

ILLUSTRATED INTERVIEWS WITH
gabriel byrne, liam neeson, pierce brosnan,
stephen rea, **aidan quinn** and patrick bergin

lot of times, just get on the train and go down, because we had a lot of friends there. My older brother Declan had lived there two years before we moved there, so he had a huge network of friends, and I became part of that.

ACTING

When I was eighteen and living in Dublin, I was going to see a lot of lunchtime theatre. I went to see a play that I think Peter Sheridan, or it might have been Jim Sheridan, directed at the Olympia—*The Liberty Suit* [in which Gabriel Byrne played the lead]—and it just blew me away. I also went to see a lot of stuff at the Project Arts Centre and at the Trinity Players, where they did these incredible Myles na gCopaleen lunchtime plays. I'll never forget seeing *Thirst* there. I was really enamored of the life, but I didn't have the guts to try and do it in Ireland; I wasn't sure if I could be an Irish actor, because of my voice.

I was living in Dublin and working as a kitchen porter, which is a euphemism for all-round skivvy, at a frigging restaurant in Blanchardstown. I was mopping the floors, and scrubbing big pots, and getting a hard time from the owner, who was always saying, "Why don't you go back to America, where you can make some money?" He said, "Are you American, are you Irish, what are you?" I said, "I dunno," and he said, "What did you come back here for? You're mad, you're making twenty or twenty-five quid a week." I was staying in a flat in Phibsboro, and then I had a flat in Drumcondra, a cold-water flat, and I really enjoyed the adventure of it. But that job dried up, and so after a time I did go back to the States.

I did every kind of job there is. I worked as a carpenter, a janitor, a dishwasher, I babysat houses—

I did anything and everything.

And then I took an acting class, and the teacher asked me to co-star with him in a play he was producing. So I started off just like that—working as an actor, getting paid. . . . And I thought, This is so easy—nobody knows how easy this is! All you have to do is say the lines as if you were in that situation, and people like you, and they pay you for it. It's not a real job, it's too easy. Of course, after that I didn't work for two and a half years, and I realized how difficult it was. That first part I played was very close to me, and a lot of parts you have to play aren't; and I realized how competitive it all was, and I got very serious about it.

HEROES

Once I started acting, I had a lot of the usual heroes—the Brandos, the De Niros, all those guys. I wasn't big on heroes, but Brando was a big one, no question, and another was Mícheál Mac Liammóir. My father had one of those records of his where he would tell stories, and I would listen to them repeatedly and learn them off by heart. I learned them when I was eighteen, and I still know some of them. Once in a while I get drunk and do a little Mícheál Mac Liammóir piece to entertain my nieces and nephew. I loved his storytelling, and it's so interesting to find out that here's a guy who pulled off the greatest deception about being Irish—and he wasn't Irish at all, he was a blue-blooded Englishman who just fell so deeply in love with Ireland that he transformed himself.

THEATRE

I played Stanley Kowalski in *A Streetcar Named Desire* a few years ago. It's a great role, and such an incredible play. . . . The most fun and the most

ILLUSTRATED INTERVIEWS WITH
gabriel byrne, liam neeson, pierce brosnan,
stephen rea, **aidan quinn** and patrick bergin

difficult part I had was, needless to say, Hamlet. The thing that shocked me about *Hamlet* was how funny it is—how much black humor there is in it. And I was very lucky to have a great director, Bob Falls; it was a very modern production that really went with the black pathos and humor of it.

I would like to do more theatre. It's hard to find roles in film where you can really cut loose—a lot of things are so tempered, so minimal. . . . But it's difficult. I've been offered great plays on Broadway, but the amount of time that they would take, the commitment—we're talking nine months, doing eight shows a week, when in that time you could go off and do several films that you know are interesting. . . . There are financial considerations as well—you really have to make a strong effort to put aside monetary things and say, "I need to do this for myself, to stay in theatre." And for me it's not interesting unless I have a great role.

MOVIES

I had two and a half years of doing just theatre, and then I did my first film when I was twenty-two. It was *Reckless*, with Daryl Hannah and Kenneth McMillan. I played a motorcycle-riding, black-leather-clad, rebellious high-school teenager who wanted nothing more than to get out of the small town he was living in,

"If you go back and forth between America and Ireland, like we did, you get a divided sense of who you are. . . . Part of me still feels, God, who are you? to this day."

ILLUSTRATED INTERVIEWS WITH
gabriel byrne, liam neeson, pierce brosnan,
stephen rea, **aidan quinn** and patrick bergin

away from all the boring people and all that. You know, all that youthful arrogant angst. . . .

It wasn't a real stretch for me. There were a lot of similarities at the time, but actually he was a very serious character, and I've never been that serious.

Reckless put me on the map and got me good reviews and all that, and started my career. But *Desperately Seeking Susan* was the first one to do very well and get a lot of attention. Des was my character's name, I believe; he was a guy in the early eighties living in New York in a loft-type apartment, and he worked as a movie projectionist and had a lot of diverse interests. He was a nice guy who got caught in the crazy situation of Rosanna's [Arquette] character. There's not really a lot more to him. . . . He was a nice guy.

I did *Robinson Crusoe* a few years ago. It's interesting that three Irish actors have played that part. For me it was just the best part that was offered to me at that time, and I had always loved the idea of getting to explore nature in that sense, in that solitary eternity. Nature has always had a huge draw for me, mainly because of early memories of the Bog of Allen, and living on that farm. My favorite thing in the world is to be in wilderness—but not park wilderness. That's one of the things I really miss in Ireland. There is great countryside, and even small bits of wood that are nice, but our awareness of the countryside and the protection of it is minimal to nil; it's almost all gone. In America it's disappearing rapidly, but there is still real wildness there in the landscape, and I think that's very important. We need that for our spirits, I think.

The Playboys was the first Irish part I played, and I had a great time working on it. When I went back to Ireland to film it, I got fairly cocky about the accent—I was doing a country fella, and I thought, I don't need to study this. But as we got close to shooting, I kept coming up with a few gaps here and there, and then I did have to go back and work on it.

I think that in America I'm perceived as an American actor; but I think that a lot of people who saw *The Playboys* started to wonder. I think, thankfully, because of *The Playboys*, I'm beginning to have a European presence. I'd like to work in Ireland more. I'm going to do another film in England now, and I hope to be able to work in Europe, which I really like.

Recently I did *Frankenstein* in England, with Robert De Niro, John Cleese and Helena Bonham Carter, and Kenneth Branagh directing. I played this mad, driven, ambitious captain—he's kind of a mirror character to the doctor—who has to decide whether he's going to learn this moral lesson from him. He's the character Kenneth Branagh tells the whole story to. So I'm at the beginning and the end of the movie—it's kind of a bookends thing.

I did a film with Brad Pitt and Anthony Hopkins, and I've worked with Robert Duvall. . . . These are all incredible actors, some of the best working in film, and I've been extremely fortunate. I'm doing a film in England [*The Haunted*] where I'm in almost every scene, where I have to carry the film, and that'll be a new experience for me—I've never done that before in my career. So I'm looking forward to that, and we'll see how it goes.

FAVORITES

In television, there was *An Early Frost,* which was the first movie to deal with AIDS. I loved that. It was a great script, and a great cast, and what it was about meant a lot to me. I was in Arthur Miller's *All My*

ILLUSTRATED INTERVIEWS WITH
gabriel byrne, liam neeson, pierce brosnan,
stephen rea, **aidan quinn** and patrick bergin

Sons, which I liked a lot. *All My Sons* was one of the best acting experiences I've ever had. Even though it was a play, it was filmed, for PBS, and it was a great role. *Avalon* was a film I did with Barry Levinson, Joan Plowright, Elizabeth Perkins and Kevin Pollak. That was a great experience. It was about an immigrant experience, a first-generation American experience, and although the culture was Jewish, in a funny way me and my family identified in a lot of ways with that story.

At Play in the Fields of the Lord I like a lot—I loved the part. It's a Hector Babenco film of a Peter Matthiessen novel, set in the jungle in Brazil. We were there for six months. It's a fascinating story. It's a long film, but it's got some incredible stuff in it. . . . It's flawed, but I still think it's a good film. It's about missionaries and indigenous peoples, and dominant cultures going into other cultures and

With Robin Wright in The Playboys, *filmed in Ireland and in which Quinn played his first Irish role.*

"Love scenes are normally diabolical—imagine having fifty people scrutinizing you."

ILLUSTRATED INTERVIEWS WITH
gabriel byrne, liam neeson, pierce brosnan,
stephen rea, **aidan quinn** and patrick bergin

forcing their beliefs on them, as we've done in every country that we've ever visited. The dominant culture is always doing that. At one time it happened in Ireland, we know; it certainly happened to the American Indians; and it's happening in Brazil very rapidly. The only thing is the jungle is so vast; but we have tools to destroy it so much faster—bulldozers, chainsaws. . . . I liked what that was about.

LOVE SCENES

Love scenes are normally diabolical—imagine having fifty people scrutinizing you. It becomes very technical: "Could you move your head a little bit that way, and could you just have your arm up here—even though it feels awkward, it looks good. . . . " A lot of the time the women are required to be more naked than the men. Me, I don't care if I show my tits, but women get very concerned about it; they're usually in a bit of a tizzy about it, feeling that the men and the director just want to see that. Actually, they have a good point; a lot of times that's the way it is. So a lot of my time in love scenes is spent taking care of my co-star and making sure she feels comfortable, and that we do it in a discreet way.

It's not always like that. It can be fun, too. Sometimes you get the giggles, because it's so ridiculous. But usually it's not the most fun part of shooting.

DIRECTING

I think that most actors, as we get older and more experienced, want to direct. I think you do it because you want to tell a story—and there are so many incredible stories coming out of Ireland, and from Irish immigrant families in America, that have

been untold. The Italians have really had their stories told in America, but there's almost nothing about the Irish. I would like to be part of that process. That's something that I've always seen myself doing in my forties and fifties. I'm too busy right now. It's too much hard work.

NEW YORK AND LOS ANGELES

I live on the East Coast, outside of New York, because everything in Los Angeles seems to be too much about the movie business. It would drive me mad. I think it appeals to the Puritan ambitious instinct in us all. You have to come out here every once in a while, and you have to spend some time here, but I don't think it would be a good place for me to live. I'd be constantly reading these trades—*Hollywood Reporter* and *Variety*—and seeing all the stuff that's going on, and wanting to know, How come I didn't get into that, how did he get that instead? Whereas in New York, you never read about it like that; you never think about it.

SUCCESS

My parents are very happy about my success. But I think that it is sometimes difficult on my siblings in acting. I completely understand their problem with people saying, "Oh, you're Aidan's brother" and them having to say, "No, I'm not 'Aidan's brother,' my name is Paul," or "I'm not 'Aidan's sister,' my name is Marian." A lot of that goes on.

I think you always have to make sacrifices to accomplish something that you really want to do. You have to have some kind of vision and discipline to work, and when you have that, there are a lot of

ILLUSTRATED INTERVIEWS WITH
gabriel byrne, liam neeson, pierce brosnan,
stephen rea, **aidan quinn** and patrick bergin

lovely, frivolous things that you're not able to partake of. . . . When you're a young, unmarried actor in your twenties you can partake of a lot. But as you get older and you're married, things change; you have less energy and less capacity to indulge yourself in all kinds of ways.

To me it's such a mystery—who gets successful in this business, or who gets to work a lot. There is an element of mystery about it. But a lot of people who have extreme talent have a chip on their shoulder, or are angry or bitter about life, and they treat people badly; and then people tend to drift away from them and don't give them opportunities.

And in the film industry it's true that if you don't have striking good looks, you had better become a really good actor, and really get to know yourself, because it is going to be harder for you. Those actors who have broken the molds— you know, the Dustin Hoffmans who broke through ideas that the leading man had to have a certain look—did it because of the greatness

With his wife, Elizabeth.

"Family life as a whole suits me very well."

of their acting. I think the film business is ridiculously obsessed with how you look, with your physical accoutrements. But the camera does like some people more than others, and so it's harder for some people.

I would just say, concentrate on being the best actor you can possibly be. And really know yourself. That sounds so trite and New-Ageist, but it is true that then you have a much better chance of having a lasting career.

And sometimes supporting roles, character roles, are great things. One of the best compliments I ever got was from an actress, a great actress I really admire, who said, "You are a character actor trapped in a leading man's body." And I hope that's true, because my best roles have been in those parts where the character was important. But I can enjoy the other things too.

LOVE AND MARRIAGE

My wife and I met in a restaurant; I was dining alone, and she was

ILLUSTRATED INTERVIEWS WITH
gabriel byrne, liam neeson, pierce brosnan,
stephen rea, **aidan quinn** and patrick bergin

In a scene from the award-winning movie, Michael Collins *(from left), Alan Rickman as Eamon de Valera, Liam Neeson as Michael Collins and Aidan as Harry Boland.*

"Filming *Michael Collins* in Ireland was unbelievable. There was a celebratory atmosphere everywhere we went. . . . There was a tremendous sense of pride, I think, that the story was getting made."

dining with a friend who had met me at an audition, and they asked me over to join them. We've been living together for over ten years now, and we have a little girl. Her name is Ava Eileen. When we were doing *The Playboys* she was in Ireland for the whole summer; but that's the only time she's been. Now she's in school, it's harder.

So my days of going out outside my marriage are over. But before I got married, I went out with some actresses, and with lots of people from other walks of life, too.

Family life as a whole suits me very well. But I think that one of the reasons I'm in this business is the need for variety, adventure, change. . . . I get to

ILLUSTRATED INTERVIEWS WITH
gabriel byrne, liam neeson, pierce brosnan,
stephen rea, **aidan quinn** and patrick bergin

live out those fantasies in my work, and I think that in a way that saves me from all the horrors of having to actually live them out in my life. I'm very happy in my marriage, and very settled in it. But I can live out those fantasies we all have without having to go through the horror of actually doing it, and facing the repercussions, which are usually drastic.

I think there probably are more pressures on marriages and relationships in this business. Certainly, if you're working a lot, and going away, and if you have any kind of fame, there are so many people there who are desperate for an opportunity, you know, that there's a tremendous amount of temptation. So you have to realize that it's not worth it.

IDENTITY

It wasn't until we moved out of Chicago and into a smaller city that was very WASP, where the neighborhood kids would call us foreigners and make fun of my parents or their accent, that it struck me that we were really a different breed, set apart. I think that a lot of kids of Irish immigrants often have a very hard time in America, and so there tends to be a lot of critical talk going on about America. You pick that up as a child, and it's a little confusing at times because you hear, "Jeez, those Americans" and the American this and the American that. . . . Over the years that changes, but before it changes you get a divided sense of who you are—are you American? are you Irish?— especially if you go back and forth between America and Ireland, like we did. That's been an ongoing dilemma, I think, in my brothers' and sister's lives. When I talk to an Irish person, I talk with Irish intonations that I don't usually have. That always

happens to me. There are times you feel a little inauthentic; but when you go back and forth as often as I did, that's how adaptable you have to be.

As an actor, you're continually in a process of self-discovery. Part of me still feels, God, who are you? to this day, though part of me has just learned to accept it.

THE IRISH IDENTITY

The thing about Ireland, and being Irish, that drives me bananas, is that we have so many different things running through our veins—we're such paradoxes. There are times when I think I have a split personality, because sometimes I'm very confident, and on the other hand I'm grossly insecure—I can't believe I'm getting away with it, I can't believe they're not going to find me out at any moment and it's all going to be pulled away. They're going to say, "That guy there—he can't do anything!" I think a lot of Irish people have a similar war going on inside them, and maybe that's why they're so hyper-critical, and then on the other hand so generous and giving.

For example, I'm nowhere near as ambitious as some actors I know; but, you see, ambition is a dirty word in the Irish culture. In my family it's a dirty word. You get told, "Will ye stop showing off— Jaysus, I could act better meself with a fucking bag over me head. . . . " You hear these things constantly, and on the one hand it keeps us very down to earth, making sure you don't have any uppity airs—or you'll get slaughtered for them. But on the other hand, I think we have to give ourselves permission to have those dreams of flying, of doing something different and wild and ambitious. So I'm constantly at war with myself, saying, "Yes, I am ambitious" and saying, "Ah no, I'm not really." A lot of the time I'm not, I'm really not.

ILLUSTRATED INTERVIEWS WITH
gabriel byrne, liam neeson, pierce brosnan,
stephen rea, **aidan quinn** and patrick bergin

In the same way, on the one hand, everyone talks about the hospitality of the Irish—"Oh, they're so great, they're the friendliest people in the world"—and we are; and we're also the pettiest, most gossipy back-stabbers in the world. And when I say this, I'm not talking about someone else; I'm talking about myself. I have both of those elements: I'm extremely, acutely hyper-critical of everyone, including myself, and yet I do have that generosity where you'll give a stranger anything because they hit you in the right way or have a certain look on their face—we're capable of the most extraordinary generosity. . . . Maybe it's the size of the families we grew up in—we're all competing for the food and the love of our parents, and yet we know how strong family bonds are, even though we find it hard to keep those bonds together. And in the same way, there are so many people in Ireland with this incredibly strong conservative strain to them—they never do this, and never do that, and never say a bad word—and then there's this wildness, this love of life, this love of dance and laughter. . . . And both sides of the character are revered, and held up as an ideal of what you're supposed to be.

It's slightly schizophrenic; we're crazy. But that does particularly lend itself to the dramatic arts. . . .

I've always had a rebellious streak, particularly when it comes to authority figures. I think a lot of Irish people have that—we find it hard to say, "Yes sir, yes ma'am, whatever you want" and just go along with things. It's not something that's respected in our culture. Maybe it's something to do with our history. Some people do really well in life doing the things they're supposed to, and it's actually very wise to do those things sometimes; but we're just not very good at it.

UPDATE: "MICHAEL COLLINS"

Like a lot of Irish people, I'd heard a lot about Michael Collins. My father used to say that he was well and truly shafted by history. And when I read the script Neil Jordan had written about him, it was just so brilliant; and it's such an important story to tell. . . . We were part of the re-making of history.

HARRY BOLAND

I liked Harry Boland, my character, because whatever he did, it was motivated by love. Love for Michael, love for the cause, love for freedom, love for justice, love for Kitty Kiernan—and, in a way, love and respect for Dev, as well, which led to the risk he ran. Whatever Harry did, it was dedicated to something greater than himself. He was never in the limelight; although Dev wrote him letters, and Michael Collins as well, nobody will ever know how much Harry Boland was responsible for the events of that time, how much hard work he was involved in.

I was lucky; I was blessed with all kinds of documentary material on Harry Boland. I went to the National Library and went through the letters and materials and read all these great books; and I was also lucky enough to meet people from the Boland family, and they were gracious enough to share their family stories, remembrances, some letters and photographs. . . . We even had some film footage. I look nothing like Harry Boland, but luckily most people don't remember what he looked like; there aren't too many photographs.

When you play a person who actually lived, you definitely feel a responsibility towards the character. And you have a responsibility towards the members of the family as well. I'm sure that for the older members of the Boland family seeing the film

ILLUSTRATED INTERVIEWS WITH
gabriel byrne, liam neeson, pierce brosnan,
stephen rea, **aidan quinn** and patrick bergin

will be difficult, because some of them still hold Michael Collins responsible for the death of their uncle. But I hope they're glad that his contribution is being acknowledged in a significant way.

FILMING

Filming *Michael Collins* in Ireland was unbelievable. There was a celebratory atmosphere everywhere we went, from Sheriff Street and Parnell Square to Grangegorman and the Wicklow Mountains. When we asked for two thousand extras, we got five thousand; when we asked for six thousand, we got ten thousand. There was a tremendous sense of pride, I think, and excitement that the story was getting made, and that it was getting made not by the Hollywood studio system but by Neil Jordan, one of our best directors, and by a predominantly Irish cast. I think that was very important—I don't think it always is, but it was for this film.

It was one of the smoothest and easiest films I've worked on. Rarely, about once every five years, you work on a film where you have a brilliant script, you have a wonderful director, and you have a great cast of actors; so you don't need to work at it as much—you just do it. It's not that it wasn't difficult, physically and emotionally, at times— particularly for Liam; it's a gigantic, megalithic role to take on—and exhausting schedule-wise. But, unlike in a lot of American films, we didn't need to talk a lot about "What's our motivation?" and "What's this scene about?" Everyone just seemed to grasp it. Neil would just steer the ship, and when we went off course a little bit, he would give us a little steering, not a lot of psychological double-talk. We just jumped in and did the job. It was great.

And Neil was also very open to us coming in with our own viewpoints. I was very, very adamant, as was Alan Rickman, about being passionate about the character's point of view about the Treaty; we didn't want to belittle it or patronize it. Neil was very open to that. In rehearsal we would share our research, and maybe Neil would take a line from that and put it in. It was a great experience.

There were so many great actors involved in this: Stephen Rea, Liam Neeson, Brendan Gleeson, Ger McSorley, Ian Hart, Paul McGinley, Julia Roberts— not to mention numerous others. . . . Sometimes I was blown away by the caliber of the actors who were there in small parts, in tiny parts, just because they wanted to be part of this project. There was a guy named Ger O'Leary who played Thomas Clarke, one of the 1916 soldiers; and it was like a reincarnation, watching him, it was like a prayer— his conviction, when he walked down O'Connell Street past the crowd. . . . There were a lot of magic moments like that. Brendan Gleeson, who played Michael Collins in RTÉ's *The Treaty* and did a brilliant job, took a small part in the film; and Liam went up to him on the set, when they first met, and was so complimentary about what Brendan did with Michael Collins, and said that he hoped Brendan wouldn't mind if he stole some things from him— and Brendan said, "No, not at all, steal away. That's what we're here for: to tell the story." To see that kind of lack of competitiveness. . . . It was wonderful.

Liam Neeson and Stephen Rea were great to work with, just great. I had just met Stephen a couple of times before, at premières and stuff like that; I didn't know him well at all. But I got to know him. He's a very funny man, and a brilliant actor—so subtle. He felt very passionately about the Michael Collins situation. Liam was a friend before, but he's become a very good friend.

These are actors I look up to, and have looked up to for many years. There was one day when we

ILLUSTRATED INTERVIEWS WITH
gabriel byrne, liam neeson, pierce brosnan,
stephen rea, **aidan quinn** and patrick bergin

were out on this farm in Wicklow, with all these sheep around—me and Liam and Stephen—we'd just been telling jokes. . . . And I was there with my mouth open, going, God, I'm actually working with Liam Neeson and Stephen Rea!

Ian Hart became a very good friend. He's a wonderful actor—he played Joe O'Reilly. In the film, Joe O'Reilly was the kind of character who was always like a mother hen with Michael Collins, taking care of him and always by his side; he was never in the limelight. So one day I decided to go out to the cemetery to look for Harry Boland's grave, and Ian and myself and Liam and Julia all had a break for a couple of hours, so we decided we'd all go out there and find our characters' graves— they're all in the same cemetery. And it was lovely, very moving. We found Mick's grave, and Kitty Kiernan was down the row, and we found Harry Boland—he just had a very small plaque sticking out of the ground, not even a proper tombstone. And then we got to the spot where we'd been told Joe O'Reilly's grave was, and there was nothing there! It was like, "Poor old Joe!" It was very funny, it was very sweet; it was perfect for the character. In a way it helped

us understand this man. We all took a photo together, at this unmarked spot that was supposed to be Joe O'Reilly's grave. It was a beautiful day.

A DARK SECRET

The Civil War is a very painful reality in Ireland, but it's never been talked about, it's never been dealt

In The Playboys, *set in rural Ireland of the 1950's, also starring Albert Finney and Robin Wright.*

"The thing about Ireland, and being Irish, that drives me bananas, is that we have so many different things running through our veins— we're such paradoxes."

ILLUSTRATED INTERVIEWS WITH
gabriel byrne, liam neeson, pierce brosnan,
stephen rea, **aidan quinn** and patrick bergin

with. I think secrets breed poison, and history's secrets have to come out somewhere; and they come out through aberrations—malice, alcoholism, abuse, lack of self-worth. . . . I think Irish people can connect to all these things. But there's a great feeling of change in Ireland; things are being brought to light. A few years ago, people who tried to bring up things like sexual abuse by Christian Brothers or priests would have been basically ridiculed; but now it's coming out, and it can't be denied. People who didn't want to see it, or acknowledge that it is the truth, now do have to deal with it.

And the Michael Collins story hasn't been talked about, it's been hidden in the dark corners; but it's such an important part of our history, and it needs to be told. Making the film was like prying off some gigantic sewer cover to see what's down in the catacombs of our consciousness. De Valera's story has been told and told ad infinitum, ad nauseam, and we all know it, because he was officially sanctioned—he was the person in power. Michael Collins was hidden; Michael Collins was reduced to a footnote in our history books, a paragraph—like a dirty pleasure. I think the film rectifies that.

Any time you shed light upon a dark secret, you excite debate. I think *Michael Collins* is more historically accurate than most films that deal with history. It does consolidate two or three characters sometimes, or put an event that happened here in another place, and things like that; but I think the spirit of it is astonishingly true. I think it's a very true retelling—from a particular point of view, yes, but you can't make a film without a point of view. It'll excite a lot of debate—more in Ireland than anywhere else, because we know the history, and there are sides taken to this day; a lot of families are still split: "Michael Collins was this, Dev was great" or "Dev was a boring old fart, Michael Collins was great." . . . That will always be there.

I think the film makes the Irish people, the Irish character, culpable in our own story. And I think that's a very brave step. It's easy to hate; it's easy to have a two-dimensional figure that's the cause of all your woes. To be sure, Britain has been responsible for a lot of the woes of Ireland; but nevertheless, you have to look at your own involvement. So many people get vested in hate, in the polemics of "This is right, that's all wrong"; they need that clarity, they need that hard line, because it's what keeps them going. It's much more difficult to admit the humanness of your so-called enemy.

That's the beauty of the film: it's not a "Let's hate the Brits join the IRA, and blow up the Brits" film; this is not a film that glorifies or glamorizes hate and violence. I heard that when it was screened in Toronto, some fervent Irish-Americans got very rowdy and started saying "Up the IRA" and "Kill the Brits," but they were quieted very quickly—not by the crowd, but by the content of the film. It shows you how difficult the violence was for the original men involved, and how they themselves were very anguished over the acts of violence that they felt it was absolutely necessary to carry out. It was not a clear-cut reveling in hatred, and that's dealt with in the film.

Doing this film certainly changed my knowledge of this particular part of our history. I've always loved history; I like digging into the past, trying to find out what made people tick. One of the reasons I love acting is that you get to explore the psyche of people from other times. I feel very blessed to be given the opportunity to do that.

ILLUSTRATED INTERVIEWS WITH
gabriel byrne, liam neeson, pierce brosnan,
stephen rea, aidan quinn and patrick bergin

stephen rea

stephen rea

The Linen Hall library in Belfast is much more than a library; it is a symbol. Stephen Rea chose to be interviewed there for very particular reasons. "The Linen Hall library was founded around the 1790s. It seems to me to embody everything that's good in the traditions of the North. It was formed by the old Republicans of 1798—Thomas Russell, McCracken—and it's very dear to my heart."

IN THEIR OWN WORDS

ILLUSTRATED INTERVIEWS WITH
gabriel byrne, liam neeson, pierce brosnan,
stephen rea, aidan quinn and patrick bergin

BEGINNINGS

I was born at home, on the Antrim Road in Belfast, at ten to six on a Halloween morning. I was the only boy in a family of four, and the second child to be born.

MEMORIES

I seem to remember my younger sister being born, and my father giving me a cigarette. I think I was two and a half. I don't know whether I just remember it because people talk about it and it's a family story, but anyway, I was sitting smoking a cigarette when people came in to visit the new baby.

I grew up in a house where my mother refused to have television—we were made to go to the library every Saturday and pick three books, and that was our entertainment for the week. It seems rather strict, but I quite like it. I never formed a habit of watching television, and it created an attachment to libraries. I think that my mother was fairly determined that we would all do things in the world.

Both of my parents came to Belfast from the country—they came from County Antrim and settled in neighboring streets on the Antrim Road. They were part of that big Irish movement from the country to the city that took place in the thirties and forties: people came in from County Down and settled in East Belfast, and people came in from Antrim and settled in North Belfast, and people came in from Tyrone and Fermanagh to West Belfast. . . . I've driven past or through the places where they were born, and gone down there to look at them, but I don't have any real connection with the countryside that my parents were born in.

THE STAGE

When I was four I played the Wolf in *Little Red Riding Hood,* and I have to say it was a major success. I had a kind of attention to detail—I knew that I wanted to be knitting rather than reading a book, because I felt that the book was a generalization, and that when the Wolf was dressed as the Granny he would knit. I remember insisting on that. It didn't come out of a long process—it was just my instinct as a show-off. I seemed to get it early, and it was only knocked out of me by a kind of adolescent shyness.

I went into a decline in my teenage years and only emerged from it when I was nineteen or twenty; I didn't really do anything until I went to university. I was with a theatre company there called the Young Irish Theatre Company, and it was our strong nationalistic purpose to revive plays that were of significance and use in terms of Ireland. It was sort of a political thing to do in that town, in Belfast.

I think my mother was keen that I be a teacher, but I really had no feeling for academic life at all. I had a strong feeling for literature, but it wasn't academic, and I didn't know where it would find its place. Obviously it found it in theatre and in film.

THE ABBEY THEATRE

I went to the Abbey Theatre as soon as I could. It felt completely right for me to go there at the time, from the provinces to what I saw as the true center—though of course the center was here in Belfast all the time. I love the Abbey and I love its traditions. There are maybe two or three inspirational theatre movements that I know of: a couple in England—the Old Vic and the Royal Court

ILLUSTRATED INTERVIEWS WITH
gabriel byrne, liam neeson, pierce brosnan,
stephen rea, aidan quinn and patrick bergin

in London are inspirational; they tried to draw the ideas of their time together with a more working-class audience—and, in Ireland, the Abbey. I think its origins are admirable, and I was drawn to it because of its place in the creation of the Irish nation, as well as the incredible writing that came out of it, from great Protestant writers like Synge and Yeats. At its best, at the beginning, the Abbey had the intellectual rigor of Yeats and the fantastic energy of the Dublin actors of the day.

When I joined, they still had that great energy in the acting, but the intellectual rigor had vanished. There's no question about that. And the way they set about improving things was not by restoring the intellectual rigor, but by rendering the vitality of the actors into the more anodyne, less interesting, more professional but kind of boring theatre of the sixties and seventies; and so I think that in attempting to improve the Abbey, they wrecked it. Now it's lost its direction; they don't know where they are going. I'm sad about that. I love the Abbey and I love the actors there—it's just that the sense of the ideas was gone.

Taking a break from rehearsals for Beckett plays at the Diggers Lane Studio in Dublin.

I didn't last there that long. I did the usual staple diet of O'Caseys, bits of walking on. I didn't do anything fantastically interesting, or anything that would have convinced that management that I was the new F. J. McCormack or anything. I think perhaps I drifted a little while I was there. It became clear that some good roles—you know, Johnny Boyle in O'Casey, and those kinds of things—would have been available to me shortly, but I didn't wait around.

Later I went back to do a play of Brian Friel's—*Aristocrats*—and I also did a really interesting play of Tom Murphy's called *The Blue Macushla* at the end of the seventies. I am very proud that I started my career at the Abbey Theatre, that I earned the first money I ever earned from acting there, and I always put it on my biography.

But I needed to go somewhere else. So I just decided to go.

LONDON

I went to London. It was the nearest big English-speaking theatre center, and I wasn't ready for the American thing. It was a big enough step to go to London. It was a huge step, really. In those days

ILLUSTRATED INTERVIEWS WITH
gabriel byrne, liam neeson, pierce brosnan,
stephen rea, aidan quinn and patrick bergin

emigration was much more permanent than it is now. Now you can go to New York and come home if you want to. But I used to talk to Irish guys in bars, and they'd all say "It's a waste, being in London is a waste," and I had this sense that their lives were moving on, and they couldn't ever get

As Ned Broy, a double agent, in the movie Michael Collins.

"Acting is about exploring the life we all live. . . . You have to insist on questions that challenge establishments, challenge orthodoxies."

back home. It felt as if they'd lost their place.

I don't think it's like that now; but I certainly felt very gauche and strange arriving in London, and I didn't quite know how to approach it. I had a huge culture shock. I think that nobody, particularly English people, understands that it's a very different country for people from the North, particularly since technically we're supposed to be part of the U.K. and to have something in common with the people of London. I found absolutely nothing in common for ages. It took me a long time to get a sense that I belonged, and I don't think I ever really acquired it. That's not entirely the fault of the English people, it's my own fault as well; but I've never felt completely at home there, whereas when I went to New York I felt at home in minutes.

But I was lucky. I wrote to Jackie McGowran, who was doing a production of *The Shadow of a Gunman* at the Mermaid Theatre, and he called me up and I had a cup of coffee with him, and he said, "Would you like to play Tommy Owens?" I said, "Do you want an audition?" and he said, "No, that's fine." I was amazed that he would do that. So I played Tommy Owens and he played Seamus Shields. Sadly, he died not long after that. . . . I had always adored his work and he turned out to be a great man as well. In later years I actually played the part that he created in the English-speaking version of *Endgame*, the Beckett play, with Pat Magee. His widow sent me a note saying that Jack would be proud that I was doing it. In the end something came full circle.

ILLUSTRATED INTERVIEWS WITH
gabriel byrne, liam neeson, pierce brosnan,
stephen rea, aidan quinn and patrick bergin

He was a very significant figure to me, Jack. Of course, he was strange and skinny and funny-looking, and I was too, and when I met Jack I thought, Well, there's a place for strange, small, skinny people in the theatre and the cinema."

I started to work and I worked regularly, and I always earned a living there. The English theatre, there's no question about it, is a very rich and very important movement. It's still rich, even though it's been cut back a lot. But then there's very little cinema, so maybe all the energy has gone into theatre.

I did Chekhov, Brecht, Ibsen; I worked with Trevor Griffiths, Christopher Hampton, English writers. I did a lot. The perception is that I've done a lot of films about the Troubles, but in fact I've only done three or four. It's not my whole career.

The thing that I wouldn't do was to become an English actor. I couldn't pretend that I was other than I was. So I never did Shakespeare. People say it's a pity; maybe it is, and maybe it doesn't matter. When I was at the English National Theatre, Peter Hall told me, "Just speak a little differently and anything will be possible for you." He was genuinely trying to be helpful, but I felt that it would have meant sacrificing something very important to me. You have to stick with what's right for you, and I couldn't pretend to be part of that culture. I'm arrogant enough to think that my own culture is interesting enough and that it contains the whole world. I'd already made my provincial gesture going to Dublin, I wasn't going to make a second; so this time I just took my world with me. I insisted on talking like this and if they didn't like it, too bad.

I never knew if I could make a living. It was a big risk and a big act of courage to try. If you come from a background where there isn't a great deal of money, the first and main instinct is to do something safe and get a steady job. But Stuart Parker—who was a great writer but is no longer with us, I'm afraid—was doing his M.A. or something when I was at Queens, and he told me, "You shouldn't be here, you should be off acting somewhere." It was the first time anyone had given me the certainty—a certainty that came from outside, rather than from some interior feeling—that that was what I should do. I owe that to Stuart. He lifted a load off my mind, and made it seem very obvious that I should go away and act professionally. And I always have made a living, and it doesn't seem to have been that difficult.

Later I was in a radio play of Stuart's called *The Iceberg*. It was a rather beautiful piece about two Belfast workers who died in the building of the *Titanic* and who then haunt the ship. Their ghosts can only be laid when the ship sinks, because the truth is that it was built out of a terrible type of social injustice. People know how many rivets are in it, they know how many planks of wood it took to build it, but they don't know how many people died building it. It was a highly dangerous job. And then I did a play called *Pentecost* with the Field Day Theatre Company, which I ran with Brian Friel. It was the last play that Stuart wrote before he died. He's missed. He was a great writer.

FIELD DAY

For me, Field Day [Theatre Company] was a way to get back home. I was working in the English National Theatre, which is not my national theatre, and I was working in the Royal Court; I was doing plays all over London. Technically I was learning a lot about acting, and I was working with great directors with whom I still feel strong comradeship, but I felt I was working to someone else's agenda.

ILLUSTRATED INTERVIEWS WITH
gabriel byrne, liam neeson, pierce brosnan,
stephen rea, aidan quinn and patrick bergin

Stephen Rea (third from left) in Brian Friel's play, Making History, *1988, produced by Field Day Theatre Company, which he helped found with Friel, whom Rea considers Ireland's greatest living playwright.*

"Leading roles for Irish actors exist now in a way that they didn't before. That was the intention of Field Day."

You know, I did *The Playboy of the Western World* at the English National Theatre, and I was proud to do it there, but the context was different than if I had been doing an Irish play in Ireland. In England *he Playboy of the Western World* was a charming piece of west-of-Ireland peasant life, whereas really the play is about sex and violence. So instead of staying in

England going through a kind of canon of leading roles that English actors would have done, I threw Shakespeare away and got a canon of Irish roles in Field Day.

It seems to me that *The Playboy of the Western World* is the only Irish leading role that's comparable to *Hamlet.* But there are a few other

ILLUSTRATED INTERVIEWS WITH
gabriel byrne, liam neeson, pierce brosnan,
stephen rea, aidan quinn and patrick bergin

roles—in Thomas Kilroy's play *Double Cross*, there's a big dual role of Brendan Bracken and Lord Haw-Haw, where as an actor you're pushed to the limits of your invention and your technique and your imagination; there's Hugh O'Neill, in Brian's play *Making History*. . . . Leading roles for Irish actors exist now in a way that they didn't before. That was the intention of Field Day. It also had strong political overtones, because the company was based in Derry and we insisted that we were an all-Ireland company. We were insisting on being part of the Irish nation.

I founded the company with Brian Friel simply because he is the greatest living Irish playwright. I went to him and asked him if he would form this company with me, and he did. He was doing *Translations*, which is a play of huge significance, and so we got off to a very good start. I'd worked with Brian before, in a play at the Royal Court, called *The Freedom of the City,* which was really a response to the events of Bloody Sunday. Brian was being drawn out of being a private, personal writer to enter a political domain. Because of the way the events of the country were going, people were driven to be public. It was very exciting to see that process occurring, because all the theatres that I regard as important have been writer-based. And if anything has made my own work develop, it has been contact with writers.

I think the company was hugely successful in certain areas. It certainly had audiences who were hungry for questions to be disseminated—questions about the way life was lived here, about why we are the way we are, why we've arrived at this situation of crisis in the North of Ireland. We drew a lot of non-theatre people to come and watch theatre, so it was very successful in that way. In terms of changing anything, or anything of major significance, I can't make any claims; but we did, I

think, take big theatrical steps that have been ignored—sometimes deliberately so.

Seamus Deane, who is a great critic and an academic in Ireland and America (and also a novelist), was on our board. He had this energy to produce a body of work in publishing equivalent to what we'd been trying to produce in the theatre.

I think the *Field Day Anthology of Irish Literature* is a phenomenal piece of work and will acquire even more importance when the dust settles over its initial reception. I don't think that women were quite so badly treated as was implied. We'd anticipated an antagonistic response from people of unionist persuasion, and we'd worked very, very hard to try and be inclusive of that tradition. I think that perhaps we got side-tracked. I was obviously saddened by the response to the *Anthology* when it came out, and in fact Seamus Deane has made an attempt to improve the situation by producing a fourth volume devoted to the work of women. But the anthology is a major piece of work.

Field Day is going to continue working. I'm going to do some theatre with them next year and Deane is going to continue publishing.

CINEMA

GOING TO THE MOVIES

I used to go to the Capitol and the Lyceum on the Antrim Road, both of which are now gone—one's a supermarket, and one was just razed to the ground. I used to go every Saturday, and if you were lucky you could go twice a week, when the pictures changed. The funny thing is, it's because I liked going to the pictures that I got involved in theatre. You want to be an actor because you see them in the movies, but

ILLUSTRATED INTERVIEWS WITH
gabriel byrne, liam neeson, pierce brosnan,
stephen rea, aidan quinn and patrick bergin

there are theatres around, so you start acting in the theatre.

I love Bogart and Mitchum now, but I'm sure I wasn't aware of their quality when I saw their movies as a kid. Now I watch their technical brilliance as actors and try and learn from it. I get huge enthusiasms for actors, and they last a few months, but Mitchum and Bogart and Brando are the people who stay with you. They restate the art of acting every time they work.

FROM STAGE TO SCREEN

I'd nearly be afraid to question the difference between theatre acting and screen acting, in case I blew whatever made them possible for me, but they certainly are very different. Theatre's very definitely about language—at least Irish theatre is. I'm fascinated by language. Cinema seems to express its ideas in different ways. It focuses on moments or actions, little actions—the actor picking up a glass—that can be built up into a big picture.

Cinema acting wasn't always easy; it was hard to settle in. The trick, it seems to me, is to let the camera watch you and to be certain that you're thinking. Theatre has changed a lot because of cinema. You don't just have to depict actions any

more; you depict ideas. It's an intellectual process, theatre, which is very exciting, and it's very different from what cinema is trying to do.

"ANGEL" AND "THE CRYING GAME"

The first movie I ever did was *Angel*, Neil Jordan's first movie, and I love that picture, although it's full of gaucheness and naïveté—I think on both his part and mine. But there's no question that you can hear an original voice in that film. Neil is not just a film-maker, but a guy who's in a long tradition of Irish writing. Had the cinema never been invented, Neil Jordan would be a major novelist—he's a major novelist anyway. I have a particular affection for *Angel*.

I did *Angel* in 1981 or whatever it was, and I occasionally did other bits of film; but because I was so involved with Field Day, which took up a good half of my year—theatre is very time-consuming—I just hadn't time to focus on it. Then a few years ago I decided that I really had to do films—that I'd done so much theatre, and if I wanted to do films I'd better start doing them. I didn't say "I want to be a movie star" or anything; I just wanted to work on film. I love it; it's what I first went to see when I was a kid. And I thought,

The Academy Awards, 1993, with Crying Game costar and fellow Oscar nominee Miranda Richardson (Best Actor and Best Supporting Actress).

ILLUSTRATED INTERVIEWS WITH
gabriel byrne, liam neeson, pierce brosnan,
stephen rea, aidan quinn and patrick bergin

Well, dammit, you want to do it—do it. So I just stopped doing theatre, stayed home and waited, and I was lucky; *The Crying Game* came up very quickly.

I suppose the character I played in *Angel* does have some kind of connection to the character in *The Crying Game*. Neil's development between the two films is huge, I think, but the difference is really that in *Angel* the character gets caught up in violence and is in a way corrupted by it, and by the end of the film you feel that he's left with eternal regret. He had a musical talent and threw it away to start on a trail of violence. In *The Crying Game* it's the reverse story, it seems to me: the guy is involved in violence and it starts to destroy him, and he finds a path through that to some kind of light. Even though he's imprisoned at the end, you feel that he's been in some way redeemed through his experience. It's a very hard part—well, it's a rather wonderful part to play, but he has no big emotional epiphany; when he's lying on the bed with that boy-girl and just says "I'm sorry," that's the high emotional point for him. I think that it's astonishing that Neil was able to go through everything with this character and still come out at the other end with an audience feeling positive.

HOLLYWOOD AND THE OSCARS

I was in New York when I heard the news of the nomination [Rea was nominated for a Best Actor Oscar for his work in *The Crying Game*]—I had two shows to do that day on Broadway. There was a great warm feeling in New York about the movie. People seemed to have taken me to their hearts, so there was a great sense of celebration among all the people I was working with, and people on the street in Manhattan.

And obviously it was wonderful—it changed everything. From being an interesting picture that was doing well it became a very big picture, and was very popular in New York. And because I was doing Frank McGuinness's play on Broadway at the time, people in Manhattan treated me like I was a true-born son of New York. The actors were really kind to me. Mercedes Ruehl, who's a friend of mine, read out the Leading Actor nominations in Los Angeles, and when she came to my name, which was the last, she kind of went "Yo!" That feeling of the actors being happy for me was as good as the nomination.

The reassuring thing about Hollywood, the thing that makes you feel affection for it, is that they didn't treat us from *The Crying Game* as these strange outsiders who came in with this funny little movie. They were really interested in the picture because Americans are interested in cinema, it's the major art form there. You have Clint Eastwood strolling over and saying "I loved your movie" and "I thought you were great"—you're being treated as an equal by them. The Oscar ceremony is like a big end-of-term party. I have only good feelings about Hollywood, though I'm sure that they'll be dashed.

I suppose what's astonishing about the success of *The Crying Game* is that a film which is so deeply rooted in Ireland, and isn't a picture of Ireland created for Hollywood, should have been taken so warmly to the heart of the dream factory. I know they talk about it in Hollywood; people now say "If we could get the next *Crying Game*, the small independent picture that goes all the way, and is very financially successful as well. . . . " I was kind of surprised—in fact it was a huge surprise. The truth is that when I read the script I thought it would be good, but I didn't think it would be that good.

Angie was, I imagine, a Hollywood experience. I don't know if it's typical or not. Certainly there was

ILLUSTRATED INTERVIEWS WITH
gabriel byrne, liam neeson, pierce brosnan,
stephen rea, aidan quinn and patrick bergin

a big budget and there was a big star, and there was also a sense that we were involved in producing a success even though we hadn't shot a single inch of film. It was being made by a big studio, and if this wasn't a success the studio would certainly produce two or three successes in the year. So it was quite different from doing a low-budget film like *The Crying Game,* where your back is to the wall all the time, you're doing a six-day week, extended days, and it's a kind of nightmare the whole time, except that there's this huge sense of energy that comes out of everyone trying to make the thing work on very little money. It's very different from the Hollywood experience.

And I haven't seen *Angie,* to be truthful, but I know that it wasn't as successful in America as the studio hoped it would be. So it just goes to show that nobody can anticipate what will be successful. If I had any criticism, I think they referred back too much to similar movies that had been successful—they wanted to make something in the

Stephen Rea and other cast members in Angel, *the first movie for both Rea and director Neil Jordan (far left).*

"There's no question that you can hear an original voice in that film. Neil is not just a filmmaker, but a guy who's in a long tradition of Irish writing."

mold of another picture. I have great respect for the director, who I think wouldn't have pushed it that way; but I think when that much money is at stake, you're under enormous pressure to keep things slightly safe, even though we know that people like original, exciting, risky things.

I must like things like that, because I always seem to have been involved in them. I mean, nobody likes change—it's painful; and nobody likes being challenged—it's awkward. But you can't avoid them—otherwise you just stand still.

I did a picture [*Prêt-à-Porter*] with Robert Altman, whom I kind of worshiped before he asked me to work with him. Altman was the first guy from the American cinema to speak to me, at a preview of *The Crying Game* at Tribeca, and just the fact that he was speaking to me was enough for me. I'd loved his movies. Making the film was a total pleasure from beginning to end. It's a typical Altman picture—there are a lot of different characters, a lot of different situations.

I don't know how much on the inside of Hollywood I really am. I get scripts from Hollywood, but I've really only done one. I contemplate others. It's a huge industry but a small town really—everybody goes to the same restaurants. I don't know too much about it; I got the Oscar nomination before I even set foot in Hollywood. I'm just happy that another area of work has opened up for me—happy that I can, well, graciously decline some other areas of work.

BEING AN ACTOR

I'm someone who always likes to work, I like to go out of the house and work, and I do get edgy if I'm not working. When I decided that I really had to do

films, my agent and friend Ginette Chalmers said that if you want to move forward you've got to stand still sometimes. So I deliberately put myself out of work until a movie arrived. It happened to be *The Crying Game*, so I was lucky; but being out of work was terrible. I'm not good at it. I gardened—the first and only time I ever gardened—and I hate to garden. . . . So I like to work; but I won't do stupid things. I try not to work for the wrong reasons.

In the last couple of years I've had a mobility that I didn't have before. I was stuck in London. Neil's film and Frank's play took me to America, and that has also opened up Europe to me. I love working in Europe—partly because everyone, Irish, Hungarian, French, German, Dutch, or English, is European and we're all equal. It's a more comfortable feeling than I had in London—though obviously I'll work in London again.

I don't know if I've learnt any lessons. The comedian George Burns, whom I worship, has a maxim about work. He said to be nice to everybody you meet and to be ready when they play your music. That's how I approach work. I think you've got to be professional; you've got to have manners.

CHOOSING ROLES

When you get a script through the post the initial response is everything. Sometimes the tone of the script is so perfect that you know it's what you want to do. It's when the script isn't so great that problems arise—you find yourself thinking, I want to work, I want to do the script, but all the elements aren't right. It's a matter of hammering out the elements until they are right. I don't know if there's anything in particular that draws me to a script—it's

ILLUSTRATED INTERVIEWS WITH
gabriel byrne, liam neeson, pierce brosnan,
stephen rea, aidan quinn and patrick bergin

just an instinct you get that tells you you could act the part, you would enjoy it, or would at least enjoy the journey of discovering this character.

I don't want to be too pretentious about it, but I don't know how you can do something like acting unless you're hoping to change your own life in some way. If you just do it to become a celebrity, or to get invited to cocktail parties . . . I long for writing that changes my ideas about myself and about the world. That's why I'm still drawn to European pictures: because normally they contain two or three ideas, and I'm pretentious enough to feel that that's important.

I've been lucky: I've always worked with good writers. For me they're the life's blood. I don't know how else you can work. I think that if you're an actor, you're dented by strong writing, and if you take it on board and approach it with the right attitude it knocks you into shape.

I never like being bad in a part, so I'd like to airbrush my bad roles out of history. But sometimes you have to be bad to get to be good; it's all part of improving. The thing is that people don't really notice when you're bad; when you think you're terrific, that's when they say they didn't like it.

I don't know if I have avoided being the Irish stereotype; people are so willing to put you into a stereotypical slot. I've played a wide variety of roles, mostly in the theatre, but I've avoided stereotypical scripts. I think that you can get involved with the paddywhackery area. There are certain movies about the IRA which don't cast any light on the situation. I don't see any point in doing anything about the Troubles; the Troubles are bad enough without having to endure inaccurate films or plays about them, or films with weary imagery that you've seen before. Quite obviously, Neil's film *The Crying Game*

took the question off into a completely different area; stereotypes were questioned at every point.

DIRECTING

Acting is a very secretive, private occupation, and it seems to me that directing is a very public occupation. Although I have directed in theatre, I never felt completely comfortable with it. But I'm very intrigued by the way a movie is put together, and I have sat at the feet of masters—Altman, Neil Jordan. So I wouldn't rule it out; but I'd have to feel ready.

THE FUTURE

I don't have any very conscious ambitions; I don't say to myself that in two years' time I want to win the Oscar. When Altman asked me to do *Prêt-à-Porter* it meant more to me than six Oscar nominations. My only real ambition is to keep working with people like that, and there are very few of them, very few like Neil Jordan and Robert Altman.

I don't know what I'm going to do next. I'm most excited about this new medium that I'm working in; I had done film before, but now I'm doing it all the time, and I find it fascinating. I'm learning about film in a very fast way, and it's very exciting.

I've no sense of "Now I'm comfortable, I'm doing movies—I'm doing what I always wanted to do . . . " It would always be a mistake to think that you had arrived. Every day is a struggle when you're working on film; every day has a lost opportunity. When they check the gate on the scene that you've been shooting, and you know that there's another way to do it but you can't think of it—it's a torment. But the reverse is also true: sometimes they check the gate and you've got it right.

ILLUSTRATED INTERVIEWS WITH
gabriel byrne, liam neeson, pierce brosnan,
stephen rea, aidan quinn and patrick bergin

POLITICS

I wasn't brought up with any great sense of religion or politics. The area I was brought up in was a mixed one, and really that's the only sense of community I have. I feel perfectly on a cusp between Protestant and Catholic.

But I suppose you're always aware of it—in a sectarian society it's something that's with you from birth. Most people behave very decently to each other in this society—I really believe they do. I think the pressures they're put under by the structures of government are very intense, but most people manage to cope very well.

POLITICS AND ACTING

I suppose that when I started acting I was faced with the question of whether I would remain an Irish actor, or whether I would go to London, assume a different accent and pretend that I was part of that culture. I couldn't face that. I hated the sound of standard English—whatever that is—and I felt that it robbed me of all color, and rhythm, and everything that was natural to me. I didn't see what was wrong with coming from Belfast. I mean, I suppose nowadays it's a little chic, but I assure you it wasn't when I started working. It was a grim provincial town, but I was very interested in it, and always have been; I'm always drawn to it. I always feel OK in Belfast.

Of course there are a lot of assumptions because I come from Belfast and a lot of terrible things have happened here in the name of radical politics, but those have come out of the sectarian nature of our society as much as out of the nature of the politics which have been used to try and change it.

I suppose I was drawn to some kind of radical politics because you can't live in a sectarian society without wanting to change it. Very early on I thought—foolishly and pretentiously—that my interest in the theatre and cinema could be drawn nearer to my interest in politics and the life of the city. And if you have any brains at all it doesn't take you long to move away from anything that smells of loyalism, because it's a dead philosophy. People are clinging to it like a raft in the wreckage, but it's going to sink. I'm not saying that to disparage those who feel the need of it, but it's not really useful to them or to anyone else living in this part of the world.

All my political instincts are towards the left. I don't see how you could be an actor and be right-wing. I mean, acting, theatre, cinema, is about exploring the life we all live, and I don't see how you could be conservative in that exploration. You have to insist on questions that challenge establishments, challenge orthodoxies. Otherwise our work is just static and sterile.

PROTESTANT REPUBLICANS

This building we're in—the Linen Hall library—was founded by Protestant Republicans, and of course the Republican movement was basically formed by Protestant intellectuals and radicals. So there are two options open to Protestants in this part of the world. There is a fine radical tradition which includes Casement, Bulmer, Hobson, Douglas Hyde. The Protestants of Ireland have had a distinguished and important place in the history of the Irish nation.

For example, I never quite understood Oscar Wilde's importance until I did a play about him— *St. Oscar* by Terry Eagleton—and realized what a

ILLUSTRATED INTERVIEWS WITH
gabriel byrne, liam neeson, pierce brosnan,
stephen rea, aidan quinn and patrick bergin

significant figure he was, and the whole tradition that he came out of. It was a kind of buried tradition, in a way, because he was so quickly absorbed into English literature. It wasn't until then that I realized Wilde was actually part of a whole Irish tradition, like many of those writers who were claimed by English literature. His whole nationalist background was very important, and the fact that he was a radical figure who was in ways outside his society was significant for his work.

So how could I ignore the beloved Oscar and embrace the horrific Edward Carson? It just wouldn't be possible.

With Jaye Davidson in The Crying Game: *the film earned them both Oscar nominations.*

"I haven't a clue what my Irishness brings to me in terms of my acting. I try to be true to what I am, and that happens to contain Irishness. My work comes out of my roots."

ILLUSTRATED INTERVIEWS WITH
gabriel byrne, liam neeson, pierce brosnan,
stephen rea, aidan quinn and patrick bergin

THE PRESS

The British press are very determined to keep a lid on anything that disseminates any information about the North of Ireland or that casts any kind of light on why terrible things are happening here. They've occasionally attacked me—for living my life, which is nobody's business but my own. And they make assumptions about my politics. They haven't asked me about them; they just write about it.

It's true that there's a war on, so the British press feel they have to attack any enemy, or whatever they perceive to be the enemy. It's a deeply conservative organization, the British press, and I wouldn't expect them to behave otherwise.

But I became liberated from all that in America. They would ask me questions about who I was married to and what I thought about the North of Ireland, but they wouldn't give me a hard time about it. It was just one thing about me; it wasn't something to beat me with.

LOVE AND MARRIAGE

I can't generalize about what I think about women. I take it as it comes. It would be kind of clichéd to say I was drawn to strong women—everyone's drawn to strong people, aren't they? Certainly arriving at functions with a bimbo on the arm wouldn't suit me.

Marriage suits me fine. I have two little boys and I'm very happy to have them—they're great kids. I did lead a bohemian life, but all things come to an end, and this is fine. I had a good run for my money.

I take being a father very seriously. It's strange being a parent—a bit like poacher turned gamekeeper. I don't like being the authority figure; in fact I despise it when I hear myself talking in my father's voice—it's like I'm a medium for something that doesn't belong to me. But one has certain responsibilities, and I suppose I'd like my children to have manners, so I have to put manners on them.

Because I've got the two children and I want them to be brought up in Ireland, I'm living in Dublin at the moment, where my family is, and I travel out. We'll certainly always be based in Ireland—I think New York is wonderful and L.A. is great fun, but maybe not for kids, you know. London is interesting, but it's a place that you should go to get away from your family—I don't think you should be brought up there.

We're educating the kids through Irish and I hope that they'll have strong roots here, and be able to travel as far away as they want to go, and know that this is always here for them. Other than that it's up to them.

IDENTITY

I haven't a clue what my Irishness brings to me in terms of my acting. I try to be true to what I am, and that happens to contain Irishness. My work comes out of my roots. *The Crying Game*, and Frank McGuinness's play *Someone to Watch Over Me*, which I did on Broadway, are examples of the kind of new Irish writing which I had been very directly involved with for ten or twelve years. There was no mad lunge into Hollywood or into European cinema—it's just that for some reason the international community picked up these pieces of work. I couldn't become alienated from my roots, because that work has come out of my roots.

That's what interests me, that's what makes me different from American actors. I mean, Depardieu is French, and he's obviously most

ILLUSTRATED INTERVIEWS WITH
gabriel byrne, liam neeson, pierce brosnan,
stephen rea, aidan quinn and patrick bergin

Forest Whitaker as Jody and Stephen Rea as Fergus in Neil Jordan's The Crying Game.

"What's astonishing about the success of *The Crying Game* is that a film which is so deeply rooted in Ireland . . . should have been taken so warmly to the heart of the dream factory. . . . They were really interested in the picture because Americans are interested in cinema, it's the major art form there."

ILLUSTRATED INTERVIEWS WITH
gabriel byrne, liam neeson, pierce brosnan,
stephen rea, aidan quinn and patrick bergin

comfortable doing French work; De Niro is Italian-American, and he does Italian-American work. You'd be mad not to use the colors that you have, because the world is now much smaller, and people have an interest in what was considered minority interest before.

Everyone thinks I'm a serious actor because I've got a serious face, but actually I'm deeply frivolous. I'm more comfortable in comedy than anything heavy.

I've been called moody, but I don't know if I'm moodier than anybody else. I think the problem is that what I think shows on my face. It used to be a problem when I was a kid, but for an actor it's not a bad thing.

I think I was a show-off when I was a kid. When I look at my own little boy—my first kid, Danny—he shows off and acts out things, in a way that I think makes him slightly different from the other kids. Maybe that's reading too much into it. I don't know. But I feel I was like that.

I wasn't physical at all, and I didn't want to play football. I eventually got involved in all that, though, because there comes a point when, if you don't involve yourself in the male world, you go to the wall. So I kind of collaborated in all that, but I didn't have any great enthusiasm for it. Now I have a huge enthusiasm for watching football, but I don't particularly like the hurly-burly of the sporting field. As Oscar Wilde said, the only outdoor sport he ever got involved with was dominoes at a table outside a café in Paris, and I can identify with that.

I think that as a kid who didn't like football, and who wasn't physical, and everything, I used to be so ashamed that I couldn't be a typical macho creature; and then I discovered that actually people, women, cinema-goers *like* somebody who's not insensitive. It was a relief. I suddenly felt, Oh, that's OK; I don't have to pretend to be a tough guy. I can actually be what I am.'

"It was a relief. I suddenly felt, Oh, that's OK; I don't have to pretend to be a tough guy. I can actually be what I am."

ILLUSTRATED INTERVIEWS WITH
gabriel byrne, liam neeson, pierce brosnan,
stephen rea, aidan quinn and patrick bergin

patrick bergin

IN THEIR OWN WORDS

patrick bergin

Patrick Bergin's interview took place in post-earthquake Los Angeles.

ILLUSTRATED INTERVIEWS WITH
gabriel byrne, liam neeson, pierce brosnan,
stephen rea, aidan quinn and **patrick bergin**

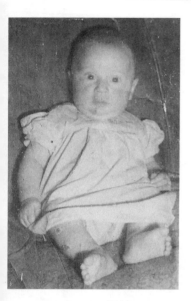

Patrick as a baby.

"I wasn't such a big baby, but my brother Pearse was one of the biggest babies ever born in Dublin—I think he was thirteen pounds or something."

BEGINNINGS

I was born in Dublin, in Holles Street. My dad was a campaign organizer for the Labour Party in Dublin at the time. I was baptized in Westland Row, and for some reason my mother was already in the church and my father had to bring me there in his arms. He told me about how he was carrying me around the corner from Holles Street to Westland Row, in a hurry, and all the Dublin women were going, "Ah, she's left ye, gone and left ye. . . . "

I wasn't such a big baby, but my brother Pearse was one of the biggest babies ever born in Dublin— I think he was thirteen pounds or something. My mother was a big strong woman, and she gave birth to her four grand sons, as she calls us, and her one lovely daughter. My sister Siobhan is the eldest, Emmet's next, I'm a troublesome middle child, and Pearse and Allen are the two younger ones.

My sister's about five foot six, but all the boys are six foot three. My dad was only a little guy, five foot nine or ten, and he used to say, "I must have been very big the night I got you lot."

MEMORIES

I spent the first three or four summers of my life in Carlow. When I think about Carlow, I think about my granny, and porridge, and a walking stick, and trains, and learning to swim in the Barrow. Kelly's field, long warm summers, and the sugar factory, and falling into the Barrow. Carlow was always an interesting town—it may seem like a little country town, but there was plenty of debauchery and whoremongering going on there as well. It was a bona fide busy town, and now it's probably one of the fastest-growing in Ireland. The people are industrious and well-trained, so a lot of companies set up in Carlow.

Then we moved and lived underneath the Labour Party offices in 20 Earlsfort Terrace, opposite the old University College Dublin, now the Concert Hall. Number 20 is no longer there—it's been knocked down. I remember going to school for the first time; when I reached my fourth birthday I wanted to go to school, and I was taken to Loreto Convent on Stephen's Green, beside the Eye and Ear Hospital. I remember the smell of the hospital, and being late for school and banging the window to get in. That's my earliest memory of school.

After school we'd go to Stephen's Green. I remember Emmet was to take me to see *Moby Dick*, and on the way to the pictures I lost a beautiful boat in those ponds in the middle of Stephen's Green, where they have the water fountains with the bullrushes. Somehow or other the boat got in there. We were about to go in and get it back when a park keeper told us to get out.

ILLUSTRATED INTERVIEWS WITH
gabriel byrne, liam neeson, pierce brosnan,
stephen rea, aidan quinn and **patrick bergin**

FAMILY

I'm very lucky to have come from a very interesting family. My father was quite a remarkable man, there's no question about it. He was campaign organizer for the Labour Party, as I said before. He was born and raised in Carlow, and among other things he worked in the sugar factory and led a remarkable strike. Sugar was one of the first industries to be brought into Ireland after the war, and what happened was that they brought in Czechoslovakians to show people how to "cook" the sugar. They made a deal that when the local men— my father included; there weren't very many of them, only about twelve—knew how to do the job, they would get the same wages as the Czechs. The management reneged on that part of the deal, and so there was a strike.

My father was also interested in raising the standards of the farm workers, who were paid appalling money and worked in appalling conditions. He was a very interesting man. He was a union organizer as well, and he felt that a lot of the guys that were working for him hadn't got the sort of confidence that was necessary to get their points across. So he got involved with others and formed a theatre group so that these union guys would know how to speak and walk with confidence. His interests were vast and wide.

He told me wonderful, simple stories—like about the first time he tasted a tomato, for example. His father had given it to him, and told him it was an apple, and then my father had this incredible explosion of taste all over his face. . . . His own father was a railway engineer, the signalman at Carlow; they had a house there called "Bluebell," in a beautiful little spot. He told me another story about how his father, my grandfather, used to stop the train, and a couple of local guys would get on

and see what they could find; my grandfather would keep the train stopped for long enough so that they could steal a bit of coal or something. One Christmas, or pre-Christmas, my father had got a present of a flashlamp. Immediately he got it he went running up the railway track to show his dad. He couldn't find him; and when he did find him, his dad was pounding the air, desperate. It was because the only person who ever had a torch was the inspector. They thought my dad was the inspector!

He was a wonderful man, my father, and in later years he did very interesting work with the *Plough* newspaper. He also organized campaigns in Belfast; he was campaign organizer when Jack Beatty was elected. He carried the Plough and the Stars against the Union Jack and the Tricolour. He helped form the Irish Labour History Society, which is still functioning and is a very, very rich heritage for the Labour movement in Ireland. His thinking behind it was that we all know the obvious people who history has promoted as the major heroes of the movement, but he knew a lot of the hard sloggers, the guys who were actually doing the legwork. So he set about writing a book giving the history and biography of these people, who were the beginning of the Labour movement. He was a Labour senator in a coalition government in the fifties—I think that government was brought down over the payment of money to unmarried mothers when the political climate of the time would not allow that. I could go on all day about my dad.

I think his influence on all of us was very great. Emmet was called after Robert Emmet; my sister's Siobhan, which is a very Irish name; Allen, the youngest, is called after Allen Larkin and O'Brien; Pearse was called after Patrick Pearse; and I'm Patrick Connolly Bergin, after James Connolly. My godfather's grandfather actually was James Connolly,

ILLUSTRATED INTERVIEWS WITH
gabriel byrne, liam neeson, pierce brosnan,
stephen rea, aidan quinn and **patrick bergin**

so for my confirmation name I took James. My full name is Patrick Connolly James Bergin.

My father moved away from Republican sentiments to become much more of a socialist in his thinking in later years, although he didn't like to use that word, "socialist"—he was a very Christian man. I suppose, to summarize, his beliefs were really about the fair distribution of wealth. But he also handed on to me what his philosophy was really about, and it was in Gaelic. He said it had been handed down to him through his family, and it goes something like this: "Is Gael mise, agus is mise as Gael, ní thigim go náire dom é, ní chasfaidh mo dhroim ar aon fear sa tsaol, ach níl aon fear coitianta níos fearr ná mé." Translated into the English, it's: "I am a Gael, I am descended from Gael"—and the next line is very interesting: it says, "I know no shame in that"; it doesn't say "I'm proud of it," because pride is a sin. And it ends with "I wouldn't turn my back on any man in the world, but there is no ordinary man any better than me."

As a child in Ireland.

" . . . when I reached my fourth birthday I wanted to go to school, and I was taken to Loreto Convent on Stephen's Green, beside the Eye and Ear Hospital. I remember the smell of the hospital, and being late for school and banging the window to get in. That's my earliest memory of school."

I have that sort of stapled across my chest. It's really what my father was about, and my mother too. She was a great influence on my dad; he consulted her on everything. They argued, like everyone, but there was a great feeling of debate in the house. My mother reads voraciously, he read voraciously, there were always books and literature in the house. He had opinions about everything. I asked him once what his concept of beauty was, and he thought for about ten seconds and he said "Symmetry." It's not a final answer, but it's a very good answer. I miss him. I could always go in and have a good chat with him.

ILLUSTRATED INTERVIEWS WITH
gabriel byrne, liam neeson, pierce brosnan,
stephen rea, aidan quinn and **patrick bergin**

CHILDHOOD

I had a remarkable childhood. When we moved to Drimnagh, we moved on Halloween, and Halloween in Drimnagh was amazing. All over Drimnagh were bonfires and hundreds of kids—and of course with the old lorry and all the furniture we created quite a furor. When we got up to the house, everyone was bringing in the furniture. I went out to the gate and was completely surrounded by these kids wearing witches' masks. They said "Who are you, what's your name?" and I got very scared and immediately consulted Mum, who said, "Do what you like."

"Maybe they're all after me," I said, but she said to go out and deal with it. So when they asked me my name I said, "Bernard."

"Bernard what?"

"Bernard Maguire." My best friend's name where I'd come from was Bernard; and my mum used to sing a song, and the chorus went, "Get up out of that, you impudent brat, let Mr. Maguire sit down"—so I stuck the two of them together and became Bernard Maguire. The next

Paddy and Nora Bergin, Patrick's parents.

"My father was quite a remarkable man. . . . His interests were vast and wide. . . . He told me wonderful, simple stories—like about the first time he tasted a tomato."

day Bernard was shortened to Ben, and a lot of friends from Drimnagh still call me Ben. When I moved school a couple of months later, there was never a fuss; I just signed in under the name Bernard Maguire. What could I do? I went to school for six years under the name Bernard Maguire, all my early reports are for Bernard Maguire. That's why they think I'm a lunatic and why I became an actor in the end. It was forced on me. Some people choose it—it was forced on me.

I've always been a bit of an outsider. I don't know how that came about. Even in Dublin, before we moved and I became known as Ben, I did have a bit of a Carlow accent and I was called "culchie," so I was always slightly different.

Loyalty is a very interesting thing, loyalty to where you feel you are from. I remember that years later I became a very good goalkeeper—I've got medals for soccer. I used to play for the local team, St. John Bosco, and I got poached from Bosco to St. Francis—a wonderful team in the

ILLUSTRATED INTERVIEWS WITH
gabriel byrne, liam neeson, pierce brosnan,
stephen rea, aidan quinn and **patrick bergin**

center of Dublin—because I was so good. But even before that, when I used to play the road league, I was playing goal, but there was another family on the street who had a few brothers and they sort of dominated the selection procedure. When I'd played all summer long for the street and then one of those guys who'd been in hospital came out, he was allowed to play and I wasn't. But fortuitously the team we were playing against, Galteemore Road, were lacking a goalkeeper, and I was sold to them for sixpence. That was my first professional gig, playing soccer. So my notions of loyalty changed a little bit.

GOING TO THE PICTURES

I remember my mum taking me to see my first film—Laurence Olivier's *Richard III*, at the Regal, I think. We used to go to the pictures at least once a week, maybe three times a week. Every Sunday you went to the cinema. But when we left Earlsfort Terrace and moved out to Drimnagh, when I was about six years of age, we all went to the Star, the big picture house. Everybody knew that when you spelled it backwards it was the Rats, which just about sums it up. Things got so busy there that sometimes we'd be two in a seat on a Saturday afternoon. As we got older we'd go Monday night, and we'd see a film Monday, Tuesday, Wednesday, and then they'd usually have two films on Thursday, Friday, Saturday. . . . And then when you got older again, you went on Sunday afternoon, and as you got older again, you went courting on Sunday night, and you took your mot to the pictures. But on a Sunday night you had to go into Dublin, and I remember they had all the ticket touts on the bridge—going across the bridge you had to buy a ticket to get into the Metropole or somewhere.

It's hard to remember exactly who my favorite

actors were at the time. I've always been a big fan of people like Burt Lancaster; Tony Curtis was pretty good; Audie Murphy was huge. . . . We'd come charging out of the cinema on the Crumlin road, fencing or shooting or whatever it was; we'd act out the film that we'd just seen. That's why, when people say nowadays that films don't cause this or can't possibly cause that, I don't agree. I think that what we see on film, even though we are able to separate film from reality, does influence a great deal how people behave and how they think. To think that it doesn't is very foolish. Movies give us ambition, they give us form, they give us in story form the moral frameworks for what our society should be like. The old seanchaí gave moral stories as well as entertaining stories.

TEACHING

I did some formal teaching in London, and I was bored to my tits with it. I found formal schools very dull. I flourish best when I feel that I can be more creative, be given a little bit of leeway and space. So I helped to set up a network of schools, in London, that would deal with kids who wouldn't go to school. I think I was originally hired because of my Irish background—a lot of the kids were second- and third-generation Irish kids whose parents hadn't quite integrated or settled enough to give the kids a stable background.

I shared a wage with a friend of mine, Alan Johnson; he had great carpentry skills so we gave really good practical, technical skills. Then there was Angela Monroe, who was just wonderful with kids and gave them wonderful support—she was great dealing with the authorities as well. And I did a lot of work with video, and puppetry, and the more theatrical and English-orientated stuff. We used to

ILLUSTRATED INTERVIEWS WITH
gabriel byrne, liam neeson, pierce brosnan,
stephen rea, aidan quinn and **patrick bergin**

get the kids to put on shows for the local old-age pensioners.

It wasn't without controversy. I remember the inspector came to our school, because strictly speaking the kids were breaking the law, and we were breaking the law—children were supposed to be in school until they were sixteen, and we were not a school. What we were doing has since been established and acknowledged as a bona fide form of education, but at that time we had to be very careful. I remember one dreadful report that said, "Not only was Mr. Bergin not wearing a tie, he wasn't wearing a collar." That was the sort of thing

"My father handed down his philosophy to me. . . . 'I am a Gael, I am descended from Gael; I know no shame in that; I wouldn't turn my back on any man in the world, but there is no ordinary man any better than me.' . . . I have that sort of stapled across my chest."

ILLUSTRATED INTERVIEWS WITH
gabriel byrne, liam neeson, pierce brosnan,
stephen rea, aidan quinn and **patrick bergin**

that they were concerned with, when in fact we were actually doing great work.

ACTING

The first time I stood on stage was at school, in Our Lady's Hall around the corner. We put on musicals, and I loved it. We used to steal my brother Emmet's stage make-up and put it on ourselves and the other actors.

When I went to London the very first time, within six months I'd set up my own theatre group and arts lab, and I found myself being a producer and director. That's what I enjoyed doing. I still do; I find directing and producing very exciting. But very often we'd be missing somebody to do a part, so I would do it and get rave notices. Gradually that aspect of the work appealed to me more and more, but even at that stage I was interested in variety. I did musicals—music was very important to me, and still is.

I think you have to find your own way as an actor. After I'd done a B.A.—I studied English and Drama—and had taught quite a bit, I did a lot of touring of the world, mainly Europe, took productions to Amsterdam, the festivals, and then eventually I worked with a number of repertory companies in England, and did tours there.

CINEMA

My break into movies came with a short for the National Film and Television School. At that time the School was helping quite a number of Irish people, producers and directors who had no facilities at home in Ireland. And that was the case for me. Shane Connaughton was making a film and mentioned my name to them as being available. I got a half-hour short and it was very successful, won a couple of awards, I think. On the strength of it, people saw my work. You can be touring the provinces in wonderful plays, and you'll never get a film career until you get the first step in the door with an actual tape. So I believe that those sort of facilities have to be encouraged and developed.

That's one of the reasons why I'm a great believer in the Irish Film Centre. It's a very important facility. And it's more than the building. It has to extend beyond that, to give a feeling of opportunity to the youth of Ireland so that they know that if they want to study film they can go there, if they want to make a movie they know where to start, and they can get advice. It's something that my dad also encouraged—the development of facilities for people.

I think the next important thing for me film-wise was *The Courier* in Dublin. I'd done some television in England, but I felt in London I was drifting very, very far away from my roots. When the opportunity came to do *The Courier*, I fought hard for it. I concentrated very hard, I wanted it, and I was over the moon when I got it. I was working with Gabriel Byrne, and Gabriel was very encouraging to a lot of people. To work with someone you had that kind of respect for was great. I was also working with Joe Lee and Frank Deasy, who had emerged from a similar background to mine, in that we had been working with local community radio, local community video and other concerns. I fitted in very nicely with them in that respect, and we approved of what we all were doing. *The Courier* was probably the first Dublin movie to be produced and directed by Dublin people; and although in its execution it tried to steal a little from Hollywood—perhaps glamour—and there was probably not enough of Dublin in it in the end, the character I

ILLUSTRATED INTERVIEWS WITH
gabriel byrne, liam neeson, pierce brosnan,
stephen rea, aidan quinn and **patrick bergin**

played was great. There was a great emotional homecoming in it for me. I felt that after that I could do anything.

"ACT OF BETRAYAL" AND "MOUNTAINS OF THE MOON"

Act of Betrayal was very important for me; it made me feel for the first time that I could be a leading man. Up to that point I'd done mainly supporting roles, which I like—character roles. But this was not only a leading role. It took me to Australia; it was international. It was wonderful. I got to work with Elliot Gould, who was great, a very funny guy. And I felt

As Julia Roberts's obsessional husband in Sleeping with the Enemy.

that I was very involved. But I worked hard to get it, it didn't fall easily to me.

I really wanted *Act of Betrayal*, and when I came back from it I got the opportunity to do *Mountains of the Moon*, which I also really wanted. It came to me with a book—I'm very superstitious, and just before I do a film something always happens to me with a book. I didn't think I had the focus for *Mountains of the Moon* until I was going in

to see *The Shaughraun* at the National Theatre. I was to go and see Bob Rafelson the next day, and I couldn't find any background to this character and was searching desperately for a book on Burton [explorer Richard Burton]. And on this second-hand book stall outside the National Theatre, the second to last book was a book on Burton. I opened it and I saw a photograph of him for the first time, and I thought, I can do that, I can look like that, that's

ILLUSTRATED INTERVIEWS WITH
gabriel byrne, liam neeson, pierce brosnan,
stephen rea, aidan quinn and **patrick bergin**

me. It gave me the focus to go for it.

Whether Burton was Irish or not is debatable, but certainly his father had spent a lot of time in Ireland, and he mentioned Ireland. There's a quote in one of his books—it won't be popular—where he's comparing certain African women to Mullingar heifers: "meat on the hoof"—this was in 1850. So he was very Irish in that sort of department; he knew the Irish metaphors. In some of his writings he compares the mud huts that people were living in after the Famine in Ireland to the sort of huts and living conditions that existed in Africa in his time and are still there today. And very adequate they are.

It was a turning point career-wise and work-wise, and going to Africa was a rebirth, if you like. It's an extraordinary place to be. I think everybody has to go to Africa at some point.

We were in the Rift Valley, in North Kenya, up at Turkana, and you meet people there who live with very, very little, and yet are highly sophisticated people. They have simplified their existence and yet they deal

As the charismatic explorer Sir Richard Burton, with Fiona Shaw as his wife Isabel, in Mountains of the Moon, *directed by Bob Rafelson.*

"[This film] was a turning point career-wise . . . and going to Africa was a rebirth, if you like. It's an extraordinary place to be."

ILLUSTRATED INTERVIEWS WITH
gabriel byrne, liam neeson, pierce brosnan,
stephen rea, aidan quinn and **patrick bergin**

with all of the major philosophical problems that we deal with. And their organization of society is extraordinary to watch. A couple of years before that, for my sins, I was the London representative at the International Bachelor of the Year contest in Ballybunion, in Ireland. I'd mainly lived in major cities—Amsterdam, London, Dublin even—and I'd never really seen society in microcosm, as an adult, until I went to Ballybunion. And you see the whole of society down there very quickly—especially when you're a London ambassador and meet the politicians, the law, the priest, the peasant, the whole shooting match. Not long after that I was in Africa, and I could see what is absolutely necessary for a healthy society in microcosm. They are able to pare down their existence.

Most of the men in Turkana carry a little T-shaped object which is used as a neck support when they lie down, and which is one of the most remarkable things you'll come across. They've been using these things for a couple of thousand years. With this you will find peace, and complete harmony with nature and the universe. You can see it in the way they organize their society—for example, the women may be to one side, with the village and the hut and the chickens, and maybe the odd goat and the children; and the men will be off to one side in the afternoon, when there's a bit of leisure time. The men get their hair done, and stick feathers in their hair, and when they go to lie down on the ground they don't want their hairdos to get spoiled, so they put something under their necks. The side effect of this, though—which you'll know if you've ever studied the Alexander Technique, which was designed to help actors open up the body and open up the voice—is to massage all the pressure points on the back of the neck, which completely aligns the body. These people have been doing this for two thousand years, and

they're totally elegant, totally at one with their nature. And they've managed to achieve it all with a little paradigm like this. Now how many versions of virtual reality will we go through before we find something as primitive and as perfect as this?

So that's what I mean by being reborn: the sense of looking at the world afresh.

"ROBIN HOOD"

I had to play Robin Hood. It was irresistible. When someone says, "Do you want to play Robin Hood?" you say, "Of course I want to play Robin Hood!"

There were problems with the script that perhaps, on reflection, I might have had second thoughts about. I thought it was going to be a lot more radical. They'd brought in John McGrath to do a rewrite of the script. He used to be involved with a Scottish theatre company called 7:84—they got the title from the fact that seven per cent of the people own eighty-four per cent of the wealth—and he was very radical. So I thought this *Robin Hood* was going to be very radical, though whether it was or not, I had to do it.

That came to me with a book as well. I was coming over here to do a film called *Love Crimes*, with Lizzy Borden, which was a film about very intimate sexual matters; so I went looking for Joyce's letters to Nora, which I find really interesting because they're very intimate. I thought our film was going to be tackling those kind of subjects. As I was bending down to find the book, a book fell off the top shelf, and it was Holt's version of *Robin Hood*. So again, this was a sign I had to do *Robin Hood*.

"FRANKENSTEIN"

I wanted to do *Frankenstein*, not least because when

ILLUSTRATED INTERVIEWS WITH
gabriel byrne, liam neeson, pierce brosnan,
stephen rea, aidan quinn and **patrick bergin**

I was Ben I was often called Big Ben, and when I wasn't being called Big Ben, I was often called Frankenstein, because I grew so quickly that very often my suits would be too small for me within six months. I was always very conscious of being tall, and trying to stop myself being so tall. With that combination I was often called Frankenstein—the monster. Not many people realize that Frankenstein was the doctor, not the monster. And I'd studied Mary Shelley's work and that whole romantic period of Byron and Shelley, and found them very, very interesting. But it wasn't until I did *Mountains of the Moon* and really started to delve into that whole Victorian period that I began to appreciate how fabulous and how deep some of that work is. I felt that Mary Shelley's *Frankenstein* is an extraordinary piece of work, and I've been lucky to be able to do some of those classics. I think the *Frankenstein* we did was a very good job. It got the highest viewing figures ever for Turner Network Television, so it was a success both commercially and artistically.

FAVORITES

My most satisfying work was probably *Mountains of the Moon* and a film I did in Wales called *Morphine and Dolly Mixtures*, for which I won a Welsh Best Actor award, which they don't give away easily. So I was very pleased with that. It was a very interesting piece of work; I'm very proud of it. It was basically about a man who came back from the Korean War both a morphine addict and an alcoholic, and he was physically abusive towards his children. Very intense, but a very interesting film. It was very uplifting in the end, I felt. Another film that I would mention is *Map of the Human Heart,* which was directed by Vincent Ward, and which I think was a most extraordinary film. It wasn't huge at the box office, but I think it was at the edge of visual film-making. And I'm proud of my commercial hits as well. *Sleeping with the Enemy* was a very well-made film. I could say that I was proud of a lot of the films, but they would probably be the top four.

LOVE SCENES

Someone said that the two most difficult things to portray in a movie are sex and prayer, and they were right. I've done movies where one is required to be overtly erotic, and it's very, very difficult to be erotic when there's so much stuff going on around you; it's very hard to be relaxed enough.

It's difficult for the actress, it's difficult for the actor. You're married, you've got a relationship—or you're not married and you don't have a relationship. There's an element of professionalism that comes into the equation, and at the same time one has to create the illusion of a chemistry. Sometimes the chemistry is just there, but no one knows why. It's very difficult to manufacture, probably impossible, but I've been very lucky in that I've worked with a lot of really nice people, and by and large we've been successful in creating the right amount of eroticism and erotic tension.

One of the great dangers is that people often suggest that nudity and eroticism are the same thing. There's a quote that says that "the secret of sex appeal is not in what you reveal, but in what you conceal," and there's an awful lot of truth in that. I've just finished three movies this year, two of which had erotic elements to them. Working with the directors, we decided that we would do everything but the obvious nude stuff and see what we could come up with; and I feel that we came up with some remarkable stuff in those two movies that is much more erotic than the sort of nudity one normally sees in the movies.

I also work with films that are not only erotic

ILLUSTRATED INTERVIEWS WITH
gabriel byrne, liam neeson, pierce brosnan,
stephen rea, aidan quinn and **patrick bergin**

but also have a thriller element—so they have to create both threat and eroticism. *Sleeping with the Enemy*, for example, was not an erotic film as such. I was attracted to that film because it was about domestic violence, which is a very interesting and important subject facing the world—certainly you see it in America every day. We did a lot of research, and the film certainly brought the subject into major discussions in the media. It was great to work with Julia Roberts, a brilliant actress who was also committed to doing an interesting movie. Working with people who are committed to the work is very important, and makes the job so much easier.

BEING AN ACTOR

In Calvary *(by W. B. Yeats), directed by his wife, Paula.*

"In one sense, being Irish permeates everything I do. . . . The history of Ireland . . . has been a great source of inspiration and understanding of my position in the world. . . . The more you understand yourself, the stronger you become."

I tend to steal from other actors. I watch little techniques which help. It's not a healthy way to learn; you've got to find your own path. But it's the process of learning—if you're a painter, you have to learn to paint like Michelangelo, or at least as close to him as possible, if you want to know the depths of the skill. So I've stolen from some of the best.

I've done some painting and decorating, and any painter and decorator will tell you that all the work is in the preparation. Acting is no different. It's

ILLUSTRATED INTERVIEWS WITH
gabriel byrne, liam neeson, pierce brosnan,
stephen rea, aidan quinn and **patrick bergin**

the amount of preparation you put in. When I went for *Act of Betrayal*, I knew the script, I knew my dialogue, I knew exactly what I thought was necessary, and I made sure they saw nothing but how perfect I was for the part. That's been the way in ninety-nine per cent of the work I've got. You have to know what you want in order to really have the sort of concentration necessary. When you're more established you get offers, and it's very easy to get lazy. You've got to find out exactly what your motives are for doing a particular part. Are you doing it for the money, for the career, or because it's something that you really want?

That's the advice I'd give to anyone starting out in acting: do whatever you want to do. If you have to do it you'll do it. I find that probably the most important thing is the preparation. Work hard at it, read, study and then do it.

It's hard work. I mean, there's no way that working as an actor, either in the theatre or on screen, is not hard work. It's bloody hard work, in terms of sheer commitment, hours, the emotional drain. It is hard on relationships also—you're travelling a lot, you're away from home a lot, and that has its own problems. I'm sure travelling salesmen have the same sort of problems. It's not easy. But in terms of sacrifice . . . I believe in sacrifice, but I haven't done it yet!

WOMEN, LOVE AND MARRIAGE

Paula, my wife, is black, beautiful, and a painter. I had my eye on Paula for a long time, but the first time I had a proper date with her was at the wedding of a friend of mine, Robbie Butner. I was best man, and I could not think of a better person to ask along than Paula. There's an Irish song that says "I have often heard it said from my father and mother, that going to a wedding is the making of another," and it was right.

I love being married. I'm very lucky: I'm married to a beautiful woman who's a great companion, and all the virtues of life are bestowed on me through being married to her. She's wonderful. Paula is just one of the most remarkable creatures on this earth.

TEMPTATIONS

You find that a lot of rock stars get into the music for the sex, drugs and rock 'n' roll, and a lot of actors get into acting because they know they're going to meet a lot of beautiful actresses. One would be lying if one were to deny that there is a certain glamour and attraction about working with beautiful people. I'm sure that even doctors have fantasies about nurses. Certainly one has an image of the acting profession being very glamorous, with beautiful actresses—I get asked, "What was so-and-so like to work with?" and I know that people want to hear that it was glamorous and sexual. And there is a certain rawness when the work is good. One gets close to the people one is working with, and very often a set can become like an extended family. I don't often get involved in that—I can be quite standoffish and quite antisocial—but at the same time I'd do everything that's necessary in order to make sure that the job is done as best as I can do it.

I dare say that if I was a single man I could fall prey to all this temptation. But one of the great and important things about marriage is fidelity. It's not meant to be a chore; it's actually something that puts form to your life and helps you through that minefield. Historically, I've been around a little bit, but if you were to pursue that sort of life of debauchery, it leads only one way—to hell and damnation.

ILLUSTRATED INTERVIEWS WITH
gabriel byrne, liam neeson, pierce brosnan,
stephen rea, aidan quinn and **patrick bergin**

HOLLYWOOD

As a child, when I saw John Wayne movies, and Charlton Heston, Burt Lancaster and all the other big guys, I did imagine myself on the screen; but I never dreamed I would be in the kind of company I am in now. I still pinch myself at times, when I'm in a studio. Yesterday I was down at work and sitting having lunch surrounded by major people in the industry, people I have a great deal of respect for. . . . And I met James Coburn recently—I just adore him, I think he's a fabulous actor—and he said, "I've been watching your work, I've been watching your career." I said, "You've been watching my career?" It was wonderful. And I got the chance to work with Jack Palance, which was a real challenge for me. That was the first time I ever felt I was really working with somebody who was a legend. I never dreamed that that would actually happen.

LIVING IN LOS ANGELES

Living here is odd. I never thought I would feel as if I could belong to Los Angeles; but I was here for the floods, I was here for the fires, I was here for the riots, and last year my wife and I were here for the earthquake. Living here is a very nerve-racking experience. The earthquake was extraordinary—the whole place going, cracks coming in the ceiling, and the noise. . . . Paula thought it was the end of the world, but about fifteen seconds into it I started to laugh, because she was speaking in tongues. Prayers were coming out of her ears—Hail Marys, Glory Bes, and ju-ju. She left two days later; I had to stay on because I was doing a bit of work. We're only creeping back now, beginning to feel confident about living here.

In a sense it's a stupid place to live, or to put down what you might call roots. People who buy houses here are crazy, especially when there's any amount of beautiful rented accommodation available, very reasonable—you can rent an apartment here for a hundred quid a week that you could not rent in Dublin or London or anywhere else in the world. In that sense, the living is easy.

One of the reasons to live in this particular place is that after the earthquake, you realize you have to be prepared, and there's a huge supermarket on the corner, there's a dry-cleaners there. After the earthquake I bought a bicycle because with the roads up the only way out of here is on foot or on a bicycle, not even a motorbike. The day after the earthquake, I was earthquake-proof—I was going around in dungarees, with my passport in my pocket. It was a very awakening experience.

I don't think I could ever live here and have family here and want to send my kids to school here. I think we will eventually return to Ireland.

We have some friends here, and occasionally you bump into a fellow Irish actor. Occasionally, my brothers have been here—Allen has been here—and we go for a drink socially occasionally. I don't drink as much here as I used to—only pints, as they say.

There's actually a bar down here called Bergin's. I don't go there very often, but myself and Allen were passing by there once, so we went in and ordered a couple of beers, and then asked the barman could we meet the owner, Mr. Bergin. And he said no, Mr. Bergin had sold the place a couple of years previously. And I said, "Oh, what a shame, because our name is Bergin," and he said, "Bergin—the only Bergin I ever knew was a Paddy Bergin, he used to drink in my bar down in Kevin Street in Dublin." It was my dad—he used to serve my dad beer in Dublin. I couldn't believe it for a minute until he mentioned Paddy Scarriff, who was one of

ILLUSTRATED INTERVIEWS WITH
gabriel byrne, liam neeson, pierce brosnan,
stephen rea, aidan quinn and **patrick bergin**

my Dad's best friends. It was a remarkable coincidence. There's a play called *Six Degrees of Separation*—and it's true, I'm sure it is, that everybody in the world is connected to everybody else by six degrees of separation.

WORKING IN HOLLYWOOD

Recently I've been working on a lot of films that were not made in L.A., though they were generated here. There are a lot of films being made in Ireland and in Europe, but the money is generated in Los Angeles, California, Hollywood, whatever you want to call it. I mentioned earlier that I've been making a lot of films up in Canada—a lot of films are being made there because they get thirty cents on the dollar. I just finished making a cable film there. They have to make fifty-two movies next year, because they need a movie a week to attract the customer; and those are made in Toronto, but the actual finance and production comes from Hollywood. So in a sense you're always working for Hollywood—very few films are generated with local finance. But I'm hoping to do a co-production between France, Ireland and Canada. I acquired the rights to *The Shooting of Dangerous Dan McGrew*, and we're trying to put that together. I'm very optimistic that it will happen within the next couple of years, and that would be a film I think we could do without actually having to rely on any Hollywood money.

Working here is a different thing. Hollywood is changing. You have the old studios like Paramount, for example, and Fox, and then you have the Valley. This area is almost like the Silicon Valley of movie-making. A lot of the high technology and the new production companies are moving down there.

The excitement of being here is modified by the fact that really it's just a job. In the morning I'll be picked up outside the door and brought to work—it's almost like nine to five.

I've been very lucky. Really, I've only been working on this Hollywood scene for about three or four years, and I've been lucky enough to have a wide body of work. I'm not really interested in being a star, so to speak, so I'm just happy to work. And there's plenty of work at the moment, thank God.

I've been developing scripts, but it takes a while. Nothing happens immediately, and I'm in this business for longevity—both as a writer, because I write scripts, and as a director, and as an actor. I'm very lucky to be able to have that sort of diversity in my career, and I'm in no hurry. I think it's important not to burn out too quickly, and it's very easy to burn out. After I first hit Hollywood with a couple of major successes, it was tempting to take on the amount of work that would make you burn out very quickly.

Everybody has a different perception of you. For example, if they're looking for a villain, they'd probably go to Tommy Lee Jones or somebody, and about third or fourth down that list will be, "Well, let's have Bergin for the psychopathic villain." If they're looking for somebody to do classical work, someone who can look good in Victorian costume, they go, "Blah, blah, blah, he's not available. . . . What about Bergin?" So I'd sneak in there. Occasionally there are a few romantic leads, and thankfully there's a bit of that coming my way now. And now people who think I'm not quite as antisocial and superior and horrible as the characters I sometimes portray are putting me in more sympathetic roles.

I'm just grateful to be on the lists. That means that you've been involved in enough commercial successes for producers to feel that you're a worthy candidate for their films.

ILLUSTRATED INTERVIEWS WITH
gabriel byrne, liam neeson, pierce brosnan,
stephen rea, aidan quinn and **patrick bergin**

IRELAND AND BEING IRISH

In one sense, being Irish permeates everything I do. As I mentioned earlier, "Is Gael mise, agus is mise as Gael." I owe a lot to Ireland in terms of early education and formation. Pride is a sin, and one has to be very careful of pride, but you're often asked, "Are you proud of being Irish?" And I was never really able to answer that question until I saw Sinéad O'Connor in concert in Atlanta. She did about three or four numbers and the crowd were OK; and then—I forget the particular song she was doing, but the song started and she went in and did a couple of steps of a jig or a reel, and her feet went up—beautifully, elegantly done. The crowd erupted; they instantly felt at one with her and what she was doing. And that for me helped illustrate how one could be proud of being Irish. In a very important sense, she took one step back into her culture and what had been given to her by the fact that she was Irish and brought up in Ireland. It made me understand what it means to have pride without sin.

The history of Ireland in relation to me has been a great source of inspiration and understanding of my position in the world. That's something I have, and I think it permeates my background, my family, my sensibilities. The more you understand yourself, and the stronger you become as yourself, the stronger you become in any field—but in particular acting. I always felt that one has to lose oneself in the parts, and I've done that a lot. People do comment on how we change for the movies and look different in every film. I like to do that, but I find that it can be very strenuous, very hard work—you tear your system around. I'm just trying to be more naturally myself and behave on screen or on stage like myself. And that is ultimately more exciting to watch than great technique.

Having that confidence in one's heritage, being sure of one's roots and who one is, will allow one that. So being Irish is very important to me.

It's taken me a long time to break the hold. And it's taken me a long time to get out of London—it's true when they say that when you're tired of London, you're tired of life. Paula, although black and West Indian, was actually born in London, so we have a place on the coast there. And we're in the process of getting a home in Ireland. We're either going to live in Clare or Kerry. We'll probably end up in Kerry, although Clare is a wonderful county. I shot a movie over in Clare, my directing debut—William Butler Yeats's *The Cat and the Moon*, which we hope will be the first of a trilogy of films that we're doing based on Yeats's plays.

DUBLIN

I always considered myself a country boy in a way, and I think that hasn't done me any harm. If anything I think I could have done with a bit more of it. I wish I'd been brought up in a small town. Dublin was great in its way, and I had a wonderful childhood in Dublin, but I think the psyche needs a microcosm to really flourish in. I think I mentioned earlier that it wasn't until I went back to a small town that I saw the actual forces that govern our lives.

My attitude to Dublin has changed, and still does change at various times. I went to London for the first time when I was about seventeen, and I saw the Stones in the park and all that sort of stuff—the bright lights, the Kings Road, Chelsea and all that. . . . Dublin seemed very grey. I just felt that the lights were a bit brighter in London.

I don't think that's true now, though. I think Dublin is ready for its time in the world. Paris had

ILLUSTRATED INTERVIEWS WITH
gabriel byrne, liam neeson, pierce brosnan,
stephen rea, aidan quinn and **patrick bergin**

its time, London had its time in the sixties and early seventies, New York had its time, and now I think Dublin is having its time. There's a great renaissance there. The youth is coming through, and I think that can't be underestimated. Whatever we say about the educational system, it's a very good education—people are literate, they read, they're probably the most literate people in the world. I compare it to Toronto, which is a great city that's also going through a great time. I've been making a few movies up there, and it also has that background of education, literacy, the arts being promoted. It cannot be overestimated how important the arts are to a culture, to society. I think because of a mixture of things—the tax breaks, and the fact that we have a great Minister for the Arts now—it's all paid off, and the youth have a vision of what's possible. And at the same time I feel that nothing's really been laid on for people in Dublin, or in Ireland, so people know that they have to struggle a bit harder to achieve. There's a great energy in Ireland. I hope it lasts.

MUSIC AND POETRY

Music is very important to me, and it's something I do a lot. Four or five times a day I'm coming at Paula with ideas for a musical piece or song. And if you really love the stuff you do, it doesn't matter if you're getting paid for it or not. I'm not a great musician, but I do feel more free and at ease when I play music. . . . With a few drinks on I can spend the whole evening with a lot of my friends who are musicians rather than actors or other people.

I have a little partnership with a guy in Dublin; I have a little shop and we sell second-hand musical instruments. And I have in the past done a lot of work as a musician—for example, I used to go up to Norway with a friend of mine, Mick Flynn, and we'd play in bars as a duo four hours a night, six nights a week, to people at sea, oil riggers, all that sort of stuff. Got arrested for murder and all sorts of weird things—we didn't do it. Mick reckoned he was murdered—I don't know whether he was or not. But it was fun. And I busked my way around Europe—Amsterdam, Paris, all the way to Berlin. I write music and I write songs, and increasingly people are becoming interested in the material. I'm allowing other people to sing it and record it, and there's also a strong possibility that I'll record an album myself quite soon.

Lyrics are very important to me in terms of music. When I talk about music, I generally talk about songs. But there's also the rhythm and the melody, and if you're lucky you pluck them from the air. When that happens, either alone or with other musicians, it is truly one of the purest places to be. A good music session will last you for a month, and I find that if I can have a good session, my voice—my whole being — gets relaxed. Acting is almost a neurosis for me; I find that music is a greater, or simpler, expression of what I might consider my soul, if you like.

The ballad is basically what I like. I like the words in the storytelling. As a result, a lot of Irish ballads are favorites of mine, but that greys into the American ballad form, which I suppose is country music. I'm very, very deeply fond of the blues. I listened to the blues all the time when I was at school in Crumlin, after my Inter, which I did at Mourne Road School. There were two brothers there, the Dalys, and they were brilliant. Woody Guthrie and all that sort of stuff was their culture for some reason, and they played boogie-woogie piano. At fourteen, Dermot Daly was playing Lightning Hopkins stuff, Big Bill Brunsey, brilliantly. And of course a bit later I was

ILLUSTRATED INTERVIEWS WITH
gabriel byrne, liam neeson, pierce brosnan,
stephen rea, aidan quinn and **patrick bergin**

very heavily influenced by Dylan and people like that, who had also come from the ballad route. I used to go to a lot of blues sessions in Slattery's down in Capel Street on a Sunday afternoon.

I think that music in Ireland is one reason why we're a homogenous people. Most Irish kids can sing an Irish song, most Irish kids can recite an Irish poem. You'd be amazed how few other cultures have that at their fingertips, especially the English. I've been employed as a musician at some of the big houses in England; and I remember at one of these things, after we'd been there three days and hadn't stopped singing for three days, this guy Kevin Beggan said, "Now, you sing." And they couldn't remember a single bit of their own poetry or culture. And that's very serious, because from those stories, and those poems, and those songs, comes an incredible amount of confidence, a history, and an understanding of the world.

POETRY

My name in Irish is Amergín, and my ancient ancestor was, if the books are accurate, the first poet of Ireland; he was the man who chose "Éire" for the name of Ireland, so he had to be the first. We bought an old Protestant church in Tipperary last year which we're turning into a poetry center, and I've been running this poetry competition in honor of my ancestor Amergín for about five or six years now. It's been very well received and I get a few hundred entries every year. There's an adults' section, and a young people's section. The poems have been very charming and nice, and I hope to continue to do it.

Last year or the year before, I gave first prize, out of sheer prejudice because I loved the poem, to a very beautiful poem by a housewife from Drogheda; and our Minister of the Arts—who's a wonderful poet, I must add—came second. Later I met him at a party, the première of *Broken Harvest*, and I said, "You might remember me, I gave you second prize in the poetry competition." He said, "I want to talk to you about that."

THE FUTURE

I hope to continue to work, please God, keep the health, keep the faith. I don't mind what work really. There's a lot of work out there. I would encourage people to join the business on any level—because with the development of cable and so on there's a remarkable boom, in particular for scriptwriters. One of the great things is that we all know there's an abundance of stories in Ireland, and there are people crying out for stories. There are probably only twelve stories, and their combinations, in the world, but the Irish have the gift of storytelling. I would encourage people to start writing scripts a lot more.

One film I enjoyed doing was a very futuristic film [*Lawnmower Man 2*] about what happens when virtual reality is taken over by forces which are biblical in implication. Chaos is ruling the world. There are all kinds of implications—the number of the beast, 666, the whole shooting match. I play the hero, who's a white Rastafarian. He's a sympathetic guy who saves the world.

That's how my career is going. I'm going to save the world.

Peace.

ILLUSTRATED INTERVIEWS WITH
gabriel byrne, liam neeson, pierce brosnan,
stephen rea, aidan quinn and patrick bergin

ILLUSTRATED INTERVIEWS WITH

pierce brosnan

pierce brosnan

The house in Hampstead, London, where Pierce Brosnan's interview took place had been chosen as a home-from-home for himself and his eleven-year-old son Sean during the filming of Goldeneye.

IN THEIR OWN WORDS

ILLUSTRATED INTERVIEWS WITH
gabriel byrne, liam neeson, **pierce brosnan**,
stephen rea, aidan quinn and patrick bergin

In the Irish movie, Taffin, *shot in the Wicklow Mountains, 1987.*

BEGINNINGS

I was born in Drogheda, on 16 May 1953. I think I
was born at midnight, I think there was a storm in
progress—that's what my mother said anyway. And
there was only me, no brothers, no sisters. . . .

At a very early age my father, Tom Brosnan, took
off into the wild blue yonder; and then my mother
had to leave. I grew up with my grandparents, in
Navan, until I was eleven. And I had a really good
childhood. When you tell people about it they say,
"My God, how did you get through all that, without

a father and then not seeing your mother?" but it
was a glorious childhood for me. It wasn't until later
on in life that I thought, "God—there was so much
that I missed out on."

MEMORIES

My earliest memories . . . Growing up in my
grandparents' house, "Boyne Crest"—it was a
wonderful old house right on the River Boyne, and
it was magical, it was sheer magic. . . . Going up to
the convent—there was one at the top and one at
the bottom of the hill, and we used to go and watch

ILLUSTRATED INTERVIEWS WITH
gabriel byrne, liam neeson, **pierce brosnan**,
stephen rea, aidan quinn and patrick bergin

the nuns make butter. . . . The tinkers—old Ma Crotchy and two boys—used to come around every winter, and my grandmother would put them up at the front of the house, and I would go off to the convent with the lads and make bows and arrows. . . . I used to tell the locals, when they asked where my mother was, that she was off in the Congo fighting the war. . . . I remember having a great fear of the world coming to an end—I think that must have been because of the Cuban missile crisis, although I knew nothing about where Cuba even was. But I remember my relatives talking about it.

I remember being an altar boy at the local church, there in Navan. I suppose that was my first stage performance—it was all very theatrical, getting dressed up in the red cassock and the little white outfit, and the plimsolls, and stuff like that, and walking out every Sunday in front of the congregation. I remember the Christian Brothers. I remember them being really fierce men. I hated school, and I remember having the living daylights kicked out of me by them on a few occasions. . . . What else? I remember going scrimping for apples at the local doctor's yard. . . .

However I cut it, I didn't have a mother and father. Tom went and there was a certain kind of abandonment there, and then my mother had to go off—she had to leave, because Navan was a very small community and she wanted the best for me. She left me in the care of the grandparents, and the grandparents died one after the other. Then I lived with an aunt and uncle, and though Uncle Phil and Aunt Rose were wonderful, they were young people then, and they were starting their own family. It was very difficult, and I think I found true happiness at about eight or nine, with my Aunt Eileen, who lived in St. Finian's Terrace. It was one of my happiest times—it was sheer magic. There were lots of kids around me, and for the first time I was in the community, as it were.

I've always been a bit of a loner. I've always felt like an outsider, and because I didn't have a father or mother figure, I brought myself up. I made my own rules, and from the pain of not having a mother there came the great strength of being able to deal with things on a one-to-one basis, throughout my life. I've always sorted out my own problems by myself. I don't yield to talking to somebody else about my problems.

My mother came back all the time to visit, but she knew that she would go under if she remained in this closed Catholic society, where everyone knew your business and where she would have been a marked woman for life because she'd had this young boy and his father had done a bunk. So she went to England to be a nurse, and strove very hard throughout those years to make a life for herself. And when she did, which was in 1964, she brought me over.

LONDON

Moving to London was a shock, but an exciting shock. It was one of the biggest stepping stones in my life.

I had a hard battle, because this country, London, England, makes you feel very Irish. They don't let you forget who you are, that you're a Mick, you're a Paddy, you're Irish. There was a lot of ridicule there when I went to school.

I went from a tiny school in Navan—seven classrooms, having the shit kicked out of me by these men who were supposed to be good, upstanding Catholics, but who were basically just fascists—to this huge school in South London, in Putney, where I had great freedom; where I realized that if I got something wrong, I wasn't going to be

ILLUSTRATED INTERVIEWS WITH
gabriel byrne, liam neeson, **pierce brosnan**,
stephen rea, aidan quinn and patrick bergin

shamed, I wasn't going to be ridiculed. I found it a great liberation. I could do anything I wanted. Academically I was very under par—I could hardly read and write. Again it went back to not having parents, not having role models. I realized I had a lot of catching up to do. It was real trial and error on my part to try and fit in.

I developed a Cockney accent to sound like one of the lads—all my mates were from Clapham Junction—and so I became one of the lads. But that felt uncomfortable; it wasn't me, wasn't my soul, wasn't who I was spiritually. I became pretty handy with my fists, because people would take the mickey out of you. I remember getting in a fight because I really liked this lovely girl—her name was Angela, Angela Grossman. I was getting free milk in the morning and some kid said something about it and I whacked him one. Then I ended up getting a reputation; but that wasn't me either, because

With his wife, Cassandra.

"She was a great partner in life, and certainly someone who made me a man and helped me as an actor in many ways."

I didn't like being hit. The thing to do was to make people laugh. So I thought, That's what I'll do.

It was an interesting situation. It was painful, and yet it was a real quest to try and fit in and discover who I was. I didn't have any role models, any sense of stability.

ACTING

THE OVAL HOUSE

My education really started when I left school, at about fifteen or sixteen. I just began to read—I could read at this point, by the way, I did get it together! I'd go to Smiths bookstore and pull down books that I liked the cover of—Jean-Paul Sartre's *Nausea*, whatever. I'd just buy the books and start reading them. Some of them I would finish, some of them I wouldn't finish.

I knew I wasn't going to be a plumber, I didn't want to be a

ILLUSTRATED INTERVIEWS WITH
gabriel byrne, liam neeson, **pierce brosnan**,
stephen rea, aidan quinn and patrick bergin

painter or decorator, but I didn't know what I wanted to do. I just knew I could draw, I was very good at art, and I had a creative bent. So I got a job in Putney in South London, at Reveniss Studios—it's still there, I believe. I worked there for about a year and a half.

Then the Oval House came into my life. One morning I was hanging my coat up and talking to one of the guys in the photographic department about theatre and film, mainly film, and he said, "Well, you should come along to this place called the Oval House, it's a theatre club in Kennington." I said no, that I'd never really wanted to do plays; I'd been asked to be in school plays, but I'd said no—I thought it was a lot of sissies, that it wasn't my style. But I went along there anyway.

It was at the height of fringe theatre—we're talking 1968 now—and it was just magical. I went to this incredible place, which was full of artists and musicians and so-called actors, and we lay on the floor and started humming, and with our eyes closed we started touching everybody, and there were lots of lovely ladies there. I thought, This is great—if this is acting, I like it! And somebody would say, "Just feel free, express yourself." I thought, Bloody marvelous, so I'm an actor at last!

I went to the Oval House twice a week to do workshops. At that time Grotowski was very big, and there was a whole influx from America, none of which I was aware of. That's where my education truly began as an actor, as an artist—as somebody who had found a voice to express all the pain, all the angst of my childhood, and all the anger towards the community, towards people who had hurt me, shamed me. That's when I said OK, I can fly, I can express the fact that I'm not a mangled little piece of nothingness, I'm a human being. Up until that point I had been very shy and very reserved, and I still have that shyness to this day. It

comes over me like a blanket. Sometimes in a Hollywood situation I'm with people and I suddenly feel intimidated by their intellect and I just can't put two words together. But you work through that, and the acting certainly helped.

The first play I ever went to see was a play the Freehold Theatre Company did at the Royal Court Theatre; it was *Antigone*, directed by Nancy Meckler, and Stephen Rea was in the company. These were heroes to me, these were magnificent. I was gobstruck.

I was about seventeen, eighteen, and I'd been a skinhead, I'd been a hippie, I'd gone through the thing of trying to find my niche; and then it all happened at the Oval. The workshops became four times a week, five times a week—eventually I just gave my job up and worked as a barman, I cleaned houses. My first acting job before drama school, the first time I appeared before an audience, was in *The Little Prince,* at Southwark Cathedral. And then we formed a company—the Oval House Theatre Company—which grew out of the Freehold workshops which Stephen and Neil Johnson were a part of. I was the youngest member. We got an Arts Council grant. Stephen directed us in a play and it was incredible. Caroline Hutchinson was there—she was a gorgeous, dark-haired beauty who died from ovarian cancer, and was a love of Stephen's. They were a beautiful couple.

We toured, and I did that for about two, two and a half years. We did some good work—we did a play by Jeff Nuttall; we did a play that we wrote ourselves about a strong issue at the time, about a young girl who stole a baby. There was a lot of performance art stuff. I did tube theatre. . . .

But I knew I wanted to be a real actor, and I decided to really go for the acting and go to drama school. People told me not to, that I was a natural, but I realized my shortcomings. Academically I still felt very hindered, and I didn't want some poncey director saying to me, "Excuse me, dear boy, but which drama school did you go to?" So I decided to explore drama schools. I thought, I don't really need to go—I'll just go for three years and have a good time with girls and see what happens. And I got into the Drama Centre, and that was wonderful. Again the education continued, and so did the exploration of myself as a person and an actor, because I was confronted with my own shortcomings in terms of plays I hadn't read. I hadn't done any Shaw, any Shakespeare, any Chekhov. Up until that point I hadn't really done a proper play.

ON SCREEN

Right back to the time I was hanging up my coat with my colleague, I was interested in films. The first film I saw in 1964, when I left Ireland and came to live in Putney with my mother, was *Goldfinger*—James Bond. Up till then I'd just seen Old Mother Reilly movies and Norman Wisdom movies. This was the first big Technicolor film I ever saw. There I was, eleven years old, and I saw this naked lady covered with gold paint, and this man with a metal hat that could take the heads off statues. . . . The next film I saw was *Lawrence of Arabia,* with Peter O'Toole, but that was still not really accessible to me, and then I saw Clint Eastwood in *The Good, the Bad and the Ugly.* I saw all his movies. I'd go in and watch them, and then I'd come out and I'd walk down the street in a different way—the transformation began to happen, I could feel it, I could physically feel it.

I went to the Oval House with feature films in my mind, not theatre. Maybe I wanted to be a film star. It was another world; and yet I could dream about it, I could feel it, I could visualize it, as they say

now. I wanted it, I guess, and when I went and worked at the Oval House and did all those things there, basically I was just a young man being an exhibitionist. But then I wanted to go on, and I wanted to be an actor and educate myself.

TELEVISION

I made the break from theatre into television via an Irish film called *Murphy's Stroke*, which was a lovely, beautiful drama-documentary about an Irish sting which took place with a lot of Irishmen here and in England. If they pulled it off they stood to make millions. Frank Satanovitch directed this and I played one of Ireland's top trainers, Eddie O'Grady. I can't remember what year it was, but it was my first television work. Niall Tóibín was in it and a whole bunch of wonderful Irish actors. It was a drama-documentary and it was very low-key; the dialogue was just throw-away, just two people talking—kind of improvisational. It was great for me.

At that point I'd done a lot of theatre, and I was making a respectable name for myself in theatre, but I was either playing Irishmen or I was playing Americans because I had a lilt to my accent. I would go up for jobs at the BBC, and the accent was always brought up. It was very frustrating. Even though I was absolutely right for the part, I wouldn't get the role.

AMERICA

The Mannions of America was my ticket to America. It was a wonderful role. It was a mini-series; they were looking for this part of Rory O'Mannion, and I got the job.

I never thought that things were going to take off the way they did—I mean after *The Mannions of America.* We had the money from that, and my wife,

ILLUSTRATED INTERVIEWS WITH
gabriel byrne, liam neeson, **pierce brosnan**,
stephen rea, aidan quinn and patrick bergin

With Irish actress Alison Doody in Taffin.

Cassie, had also done a Bond movie, *For Your Eyes Only,* and that job came at a point when we had hardly any bloody money. So with the proceeds from her salary and my salary we bought a home in Wimbledon. And by this time, when the mini-series was coming on TV in America, we had bought the house. She said, "We really should go to America to be seen." I said that we had no money, how the hell were we to get to bloody America? She said not to worry, that she would find a way. And she did; she took out a second mortgage on the central heating. We applied, went to the bank manager, got two thousand quid. Then we had to go through the

ILLUSTRATED INTERVIEWS WITH
**gabriel byrne, liam neeson, pierce brosnan,
stephen rea, aidan quinn and patrick bergin**

whole formality of the central heating people coming round, and hiding the radiators. . . .

Anyway, thanks to Freddie Laker we went over there just when *Mannions of America* came on TV. I got an agent in those two weeks, and he put us up in his back room; I rented a car from Rent-a-Wreck, which is an old company in America, and I went and saw everybody in town. Zoetrope—Coppola's firm— was going then, and I distinctly remember going there. And for the very first interview I had in America, I drove over Laurel Canyon. I thought, Jesus, here I am in America, going over Laurel Canyon!

The first job I went for was *Remington Steele*. If I hadn't got *Remington* I would have been in the hole for a lot of money. It would have meant coming back to Britain, and having to really work my tail off to pay back the two thousand pounds. That was a lot of money.

They asked me if I'd be prepared to move over to the States. And I said sure, absolutely. "You've got a family?" "That's no problem." I felt at home, once I got off that plane in America. I felt connected— with the country, the openness of the people. Ambition wasn't a dirty word here; wanting to be successful was not something to be ashamed of. And there was an acceptance of me as a man, as an actor. . . . I just felt very at home.

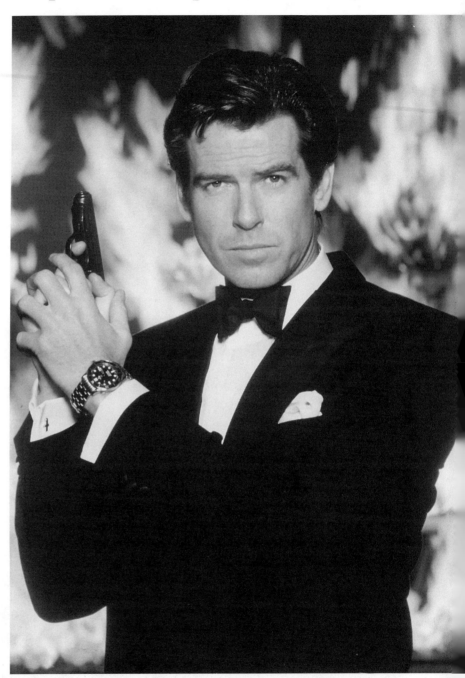

As Bond, James Bond, in Goldeneye.

ILLUSTRATED INTERVIEWS WITH
gabriel byrne, liam neeson, **pierce brosnan**,
stephen rea, aidan quinn and patrick bergin

I felt lucky and I was lucky—I mean, I got this job, which was unbelievable.

So I spent two weeks there and the mini-series came out. Then they interviewed me again, and they asked the same questions. We went back to England and then they asked me back to Los Angeles, I did the pilot, and it got picked up for nine episodes.

So Cassie, the children and I packed up our bags and went to Hollywood. And then it went from nine episodes to thirteen, to twenty-two, and in the end I spent five years doing it. It's destiny—if a door opens for you, you have to go through it. If you hesitate, if you're not prepared for it, the door closes.

BOND

I was offered Bond in '86. *Remington* was cancelled and they offered me the role, and I said yes. But I had this little sixty-day clause in the contract with MGM—they had sixty days in which to re-sell it. During those sixty days the negotiations for my contract had started. I had done the wardrobe fittings, my stunt double had started in Gibraltar on the movie. But on the sixtieth day it all went in the toilet. Basically what happened was that Cubby Broccoli said to them, "Look, you can have him for six episodes but no more," and they said, "Let's wait and see, let's discuss this." That was Day 57 or 58. And on the sixtieth day, at 6:30 in the evening, they came back to my agents and United Artists, and they said, "We'll give him to you for the six episodes, but we want the option on twenty-two." Meaning do the six, do James Bond and then go back to *Remington Steele*—greed. . . . Very short-sighted people, certain people at the network.

I had to do the six episodes of *Remington Steele,* and we canceled it. Actors lose jobs every day,

fine, wonderful jobs that can make your career, that can make you a household name, that can help you buy a bigger house or put you on the map. This was one of those jobs in my career. It just came with such media attention and such hoopla that I felt very manipulated and very impotent.

I never thought I'd get a chance at Bond again. I kissed it goodbye. It was a real sucker punch and I know that Cassie took it very hard, in the sense that you do for your partner in life. If somebody is hurting your wife, if your wife's having a hard time, you want to throttle them. She was just livid, and I would placate her and say, "Listen, don't worry about it—it just wasn't meant to be, somebody up there just doesn't want us to do it . . ."

I certainly wasn't waiting in the wings for it to come back into my life; I was happy getting on with my career. But I find it's amazing that Bond has always been in my life—from 1964 when I saw *Goldfinger* as a young boy, to Cassie being in *For Your Eyes Only*, to being offered it in '86, to being denied it, then having it come back in again.

MOVIES

My first film was *The Long Good Friday*, with Bob Hoskins. I played the IRA hitman. I had no idea what the story was about, they never sent me a script or anything—I just had to show up at the swimming pool one morning, and kind of pick this guy up, and go to kiss him and then stab him. But it was a memorable little performance because he was the noises off, as it were, and I was part of this wonderful ensemble, and it was a great film.

After *Remington Steele* I had a fight on my hands. I felt that I was going to have to prove myself, to prove that I could make it into movies and not be seen as some kind of "pretty boy," or whatever, but

ILLUSTRATED INTERVIEWS WITH
gabriel byrne, liam neeson, **pierce brosnan**,
stephen rea, aidan quinn and patrick bergin

as someone of substance. My work started as substance—I'm a peasant at heart, I'm not a bloody leading man. I saw myself as a character actor, as a man with dirt under the nails. *Remington* was just something I did and seemed to do pretty well. And it captured people's imaginations—tags like "the next Cary Grant" got put on you.

But I've always been very, very fortunate. *Remington Steele* was wonderful, the Bond episode happened and then I just went off and did a mini-series straight after, called *Noble House*. I hadn't read the book, I'd never seen *Shogun*—I knew *Shogun* was a big success—but I was so pissed off with all the proceedings I just said "Yes, I'll do it." People asked me if I had read the book. I tried to read the book, but I couldn't. It was just that I was so angry with other things. James Clavell is a wonderful writer, very entertaining, but I just couldn't get my head around it.

Sometimes you don't need to read the bloody book anyway. If it's in the script, that's all you need. People ask you what you do as preparation—just read the bloody script. If it's a well-written script, if the character is there, then you don't have to go off and beat yourself up. That's not my style. You just sit back and have a quiet jar somewhere, and just let your mind ramble—just imagine it.

So I did that in Hong Kong, that was wonderful. Then I did a little film in Ireland which I loved, called *Taffin*, with the late great Ray MacAnally and Patrick Bergin. Patrick Bergin played my brother. That was lovely; that was a great time, about seven or eight weeks in Ireland, in Wicklow.

The first Hollywood movie I did was called *Nomads*, with Lesley-Anne Down. It was John McTiernan's first film from the American Film Institute. It's a very good film—it's a good psychological thriller. I play this French anthropologist who's haunted by

the Inuit, who are Eskimos; he lives on an ice floe and they get invaded by the spirits. John did a great job on it, and I did a pretty damn good job myself, actually—wasn't bad. But it didn't go anywhere. It certainly launched his bloody career, that's for sure, because he did *Predator* right after that.

The Fourth Protocol was in '86, the year of Bond being in my life. It was amazing. Michael Caine and I were filming up in Peterborough and the press were all over the set for me because they thought I was going to be the next Bond. But *The Fourth Protocol* was good. It was the second time I worked with John McKenzie, after *The Long Good Friday,* where I didn't say a bloody word, I just went round killing guys. *The Fourth Protocol* was more or less the same, except I was a Russian killing people, picking people up again—boys and girls—and nailing them.

Lawnmower Man came into my life at a great time. It was just a script that came through the door and I really needed the money at the time. And it was one of those things that you read and you think, *Lawnmower Man*? Who's pulling my chain here? Oh, OK, I'll do it. . . . I met with Brett Leonard, who's a really great director, lovely fella, and we became good friends. And we just started filming it, and the more I got into it and the more I began to educate myself about virtual reality, the more I realized that I'd hit the little pot of gold with the movie. It became a cult film.

I was very content with the way my career was going. After *Mrs. Doubtfire*, I found I really had a toe in the door with the studios. I got this film with Warren Beatty—*Love Affair*—which didn't do very well in America, unfortunately; but I thought at last, I'd taken a risk there.

The year before last I didn't do any television;

ILLUSTRATED INTERVIEWS WITH
gabriel byrne, liam neeson, **pierce brosnan**,
stephen rea, aidan quinn and patrick bergin

With partner Keely Shaye-Smith, his mother, May Carmichael, his son Christopher and daughter Charlotte.

"My mother has always been very supportive. . . . When I said I wanted to be an actor, she was right behind me."

I didn't make any bloody money either, but I thought I'll hold out for feature films. I was watching Liam take off, and I thought Jesus, great, and I saw Gabriel take off, and I saw *The Crying Game* and I saw Stephen take off, and I saw Patrick Bergin take off; and I thought, Jesus Christ, I was out here before the lot of them, doing fucking *Remington Steele*. I certainly didn't wish the fellas ill will, though. But here I am now with Bond, which is powerful stuff, and there's an audience there for it.

I did *Robinson Crusoe* in Papua New Guinea. There was a certain element of introspectiveness; it was pretty lonely in the sense that you are the only actor on the call sheet in the morning, and it's just you and a film crew in the jungle of Papua New Guinea. But I didn't become so introspective that it became painful, or that I became adrift from myself or from the character. I certainly used some of my aloneness in life for this character. Irony of ironies, it's been played before by two Irishmen: Dan O'Herlihy, who was nominated for an Oscar, and Aidan Quinn.

We didn't have a lot of time on this project— it started as a CBS two-hour movie. I'd always loved the story. I can't say it was a story I grew up reading as a young boy, because books never played a part in my childhood; but it is a book that I've read to Sean, when he was younger—he's eleven now—so I was delighted to do it. I did it as a CBS special, but then Bond came into my life, and lo and behold, it went from being a two-hour TV movie to a film for Miramax. Harvey Weinstein, clever lad that he is, said, "Hang on, we could make money here, let's buy this." I believe what we put down was good, but we didn't have enough time; and when you have a hybrid like a TV production which becomes a film, it's a hard transformation.

But it was a good experience to make it. I played Crusoe as this Scottish Calvinist who was really very at one with his God. He rules his life by the Bible and his God, so when he meets this heathen, this savage, it becomes a real stand-off between the two men. It is not an easy relationship. It was a good film, and I'm pretty proud of the work.

ADVICE

I'd tell anyone starting out as an actor to read as much as possible—read anything you can get your hands on. Educate yourself. Read the classics.

Be bold. Push yourself; have no fear, take a big breath and just jump off. Go out there and grab it by the throat. It takes a lot of courage to act, it really does. It doesn't get any easier. On my first day of shooting for *Goldeneye,* Robbie Coltrane was sitting there and I'm here with my heart beating like crazy; but you can't let them see that, so you have to learn techniques to cover that, veil that. You feel very lonely and this beast is on you, and the clapper goes "Show me what you've got". . . . Try to be relaxed, try to be cool—just try to do it.

CASSIE

Cassie and I met through an Irishman, David Harris, who was one of the Harris clan. He was at drama school with me. When we finished drama school, I was living in Fulham and he was living round the corner from me, in Cassie's house. By this time Cassie's marriage to Dermot Harris—Richard Harris's brother—was over; she'd taken the two young children and gone into the night to start a life for herself. So David Harris said, "Come round and we'll go out for a pint and play snooker"—I used to play at the Putney Bridge snooker hall. And I went round there one day and she came down the stairs—she'd just been away filming a film with Burt Reynolds

called *Rough Cut*, or something like that. She came down the stairs, and that was the first time I saw her.

I said, "Who's that?"

David said, "That's my aunt."

I said, "That can't be your bloody aunt—get out of here—she's gorgeous!"

She was just magnificent, a beautiful woman. And it certainly wasn't love at first sight on her part, but it was on mine. I mean that was it, really; it just started from there.

I was a bit heavier then, Guinness and stuff like that, and I was in a play called *Philomena* and I was playing McCaley, who was the plumber, so I had this short back and sides—so I looked like a complete wally. I thought I was the bee's knees. I was very arrogant in those days, very full of myself. Jesus, how the hell did she ever fall for me?

It took a while. I would go round quite a lot. I used to go round on my bicycle, pedal around furiously, get off panting. . . . She had a party one night and she invited a lot of people, but it was the night of the World Cup—she didn't take that into consideration. Everybody stayed home watching the World Cup, but I was there. I was never big into soccer.

It was just magic. I mean, the first night we spent together I thought, This woman doesn't want to be with me. I got on the bike the next morning and rode off back to the flat and I thought, What am I doing? It's total lunacy—this is a beautiful woman, she's got children, she doesn't want to be with me. I better phone—no I won't, no, I won't make a fool of myself. . . . A couple of days went by. I phoned up and she asked me round for a cup of tea. It was very shy on both our parts.

I invited quite a few people to the theatre that night, but I didn't invite her. David Harris came to the play, and afterwards we were in the pub, and I

ILLUSTRATED INTERVIEWS WITH
gabriel byrne, liam neeson, **pierce brosnan**,
stephen rea, aidan quinn and patrick bergin

said that I really liked her a lot. He asked me why I hadn't invited her to the play. I said, "I didn't think she'd want to come."

"You're so thick," he said. "She's waiting for you."

I put the pint down, I went out into Piccadilly Circus, I got in a cab, stopped off in the apartment on the way home, got a bottle of champagne, went round there. The light was on in the bedroom. I thought, Oh God, rang the doorbell—no answer. Rang the doorbell again, no answer; I walked away thinking I really had made a fool of myself. I decided I was going to sit on the doorstep until she came back. Actually, she was doing an interview with John Hurt for *Cosmopolitan* magazine; and David had phoned her up in the restaurant and said "He's on his way over." She stopped the interview, ran round, and as I was walking down the street, she was walking up the street, and it was just gorgeous. We just walked and walked until we met, and then we never left each other's side, really.

We moved in together; she got rid of that house and came to stay in my little flat. Cassie and her two beautiful children, Charlotte and Christopher—they were like three and four. . . . I never really thought, Oh my God, this woman's got two kids; I just fell madly in love with her and had great fun at the same time. Suddenly, I had this wonderful lady, and she just happened to have two kids, and I became a father. I suppose not having a father gave me certain gifts—a certain awareness, a flexibility of heart and mind.

Then we rented a house together and the adventure began. . . .

When I did *The Deceivers*, Cassie came to India with me. She felt sick when she was getting on the plane, but she still came to India. She felt very lousy during the stay in India. Six months before, her gynecologist had said that one of her ovaries had dropped, but told her not to worry about it, that it was OK, very normal. We came back from India just before Christmas '87, and discovered that she had ovarian cancer.

Life went kaput. We stayed in London for a while and then went back to America and started tackling ovarian cancer. I had to work, though, as well. I did a mini-series called *Around the World in 80 Days*, which was very difficult because Cassie was having lots of operations, but she told me to go. I mean, you have to work, you have to pay the rent. The children were at private school here in England. I took some time off to be with her, and then the money would run out and I had to go off again. I did a film called *Mister Johnson*, in Nigeria. . . .

And it was so hard. Four years she lived with it, it took her four years to die—and yet you can taste life so much when you're living with death. We never talked about dying, really. She had such an incredible spirit—the cup for her was always half full. I mean, we bought and sold and bought a house during that time, and selling and buying a house is always tough even when you're in full health, never mind dealing with ovarian cancer. She always thought she was going to whip it.

I think my protective instinct towards women came from seeing Cassie go through her cancer, and watching a life dwindle down before me—a beautiful life, and a beautiful woman, and a great friend and companion. To see her strength and courage being undermined by a disgusting, insidious disease. . . . I felt so powerless to do anything. She was so bright and intelligent—sitting in doctors' waiting rooms, she would be the one to ask the questions I was too scared to ask. How long? What if? Why? How? Yes, I want to do radiation because my investigations have told me what happens with radiation, I'll do this chemotherapy, I won't do this

ILLUSTRATED INTERVIEWS WITH
gabriel byrne, liam neeson, **pierce brosnan**,
stephen rea, aidan quinn and patrick bergin

chemotherapy. . . .

There was a lot of anger with the diagnosis—why didn't he investigate? why didn't he go in?—but you have to let that go; otherwise it just deepens the pain and gets you nowhere. You have to get on with your life, make each day the best. You have children, three children—how do you make it great for them? The children have been magnificent, and I've watched Charlotte and Christopher live through it and become very beautiful and wonderful and loving, caring. Likewise Sean.

She died before Bond came back into my life again. She would have loved this. It was great stepping out together; she was such a beauty, she had such a love of people and life. She was a great partner in life, and certainly someone who made me a man and helped me as an actor in many ways. This business is so full of nonsense. It's a simple job to do, really: you go out there and you do it well, or you don't do it too well; you get the job, or you don't get the job. She was a great leveller in my life.

I heard this theory that when you're diagnosed with cancer, you can usually see that something traumatic happened eighteen months before the diagnosis. When Cassie looked back eighteen months, the trauma was my not getting James Bond. It's an old wives' tale, maybe. Cassie's mother died from ovarian cancer, and they feel that it is hereditary. My daughter, Charlotte, who's twenty-three—a young woman—lives under the shadow of this now, so she is checked out every six months.

I have done work for various causes and I have spoken in front of Congress about the shameful neglect of women's health care in America. I was asked to do it—I didn't want to do it, but then I thought, Well, hang on a sec—I've just lived through this. I've been quiet, I've watched a beautiful life dwindle down. It's my responsibility to speak out. I'm in a position to speak maybe for other men, not in a grandiose way, but just humbly, simply. This is my story and these are the pitfalls; this was the diagnosis; and this was our journey from one doctor to the next, one city to the next, trying to find a cure, to save a life. It's been therapeutic, and I still lend my name. Before Cassie got cancer I'd been to so many bloody black-tie events for cancer, and it just appalled me. Where does the money go? I'd seen millions being made. Does this money get to the source? Why is this disease still in our society anyway?

It was a great, great loss, a frightening loss. There's a lot of guilt that goes with it, a lot of pain—"I could've done more, I should've done this, why didn't I speak up in the doctor's?" And there's anger there still, though somewhat less now. It's a great shock—the pain of seeing it happen before you, of going through to that great last moment, which is so simple: you breathe in, you breathe out, you breathe in, you breathe out, and that's it. . . .

She never wanted to die—no one wants to die. And we never talked about it until near the end. I remember one day I was in the studio, painting, and I could hear her down in the kitchen on the phone to the doctor, and I just kept on painting, kept on painting, don't think, don't think. And she came up and she walked behind me and sat down, and I was painting away, just. . . . And I said, "Are you all right?" and she said, "It doesn''t look too good for me." Those were the first heavy words spoken by her. And we just sat there and held each other and wept, and then it was, "OK, right, let's have some lunch . . ."—what else can you talk about?

You really feel your soul, your heart deepen, and you feel another level of life. I felt myself grow as a man, become a bit wiser, a bit more weary with it, and also exhilarated by life at the same time,

ILLUSTRATED INTERVIEWS WITH
gabriel byrne, liam neeson, **pierce brosnan**,
stephen rea, aidan quinn and patrick bergin

because you just live in the moment. It certainly has marked me, but in a good way—there's a great gift to be had from sharing it. She showed me so much in life, and she showed me how to die with grace and how to live with grace and how to embrace this life.

She didn't want to leave Sean; she wanted to see him grow up. I found a letter afterwards—that was a tough find, just a letter written on her yellow notepad to me. . . .

I find it tough being without her as a man—to be out there as a forty-one-year-old man in the world again, to be available, as it were, to find that partner again, to have relationships with women. It's exciting, it's great—I've met some wonderful women, and I've made some wonderful relationships—but. . . . When she died I thought, Well, here I go again, I feel like that boy of eleven years old who came to England. I feel like that boy of six who's walking the streets of Kells and whose mother has just gone on the plane back to England.

But it's all good stuff, it's great, if you know how to look at it in the right way and not get sentimental and maudlin about it. That's easy to do, but you have to smack yourself out of it and ask yourself how you use that pain in your work, be it painting or writing or acting. You take all that pain and you put it back into the work, and you take your children by the hand and sit there with them. I'm glad that I'm there for them and they're there for me, to help each other to look life in the eye. And it's a great life, it's wonderful, it's a great journey.

FAMILY RELATIONSHIPS

As a little boy I yearned to have a family. I guess I saw families around me, but I also saw the pain from my mother as well—she would come home every year from England, and there was pain on both sides of the fence there. It wasn't until I went and did *Remington Steele* later on in life, and I started becoming famous and people asked me about my life and I saw some of the things I said in print, that I realized how much pain was there. I kind of opened my big mouth in the beginning because I was unused to the media. And then I saw how it hurt my mother and hurt my relatives back in Ireland. It wasn't intentional—it was just telling my story.

My mother has always been very supportive. She experienced such great loss during the early fifties, but now she and I have created a life for ourselves. When I said I wanted to be an actor, she was right behind me. And we get on really well now, even though for those lost years certain parts of the jigsaw have been left out.

I'd love to have known my father, Tom. I met him once. When I went back to do *Remington Steele,* the storyline had reached a certain point and we used a bit of my background in the sense that Remington never knew who his father was. I said that we should go to Ireland and that my character should try to look up his father. And of course, when we were there, Tom Brosnan came back into my life. I was staying at the Berkeley Court, and Tom came up one Sunday afternoon.

It was strange. There was a knock on the door and when I opened it, there was Tom, this wonderful Kerryman. "Ah, Jaysus, you look handsome, very handsome, oh yes, . . ." We sat down and had tea and we chatted for a while, but there was so much of life that had been missed. And he came with about six first cousins who I had never seen; and it was difficult, it was a difficult meeting, because I was working a six-day week and I could only see him on that Sunday. But we did meet, and there was still a lot of patching up to be done . . .

ILLUSTRATED INTERVIEWS WITH
gabriel byrne, liam neeson, **pierce brosnan**,
stephen rea, aidan quinn and patrick bergin

In Mrs. Doubtfire, *1993, starring Robin Williams.*

"I've kept journals throughout my life . . . maybe I'll find some way to tell these Irish stories in print. There's lots of imagery there which is so richly lyrical, so funny."

THE FUTURE

I'd like to write. I do write, I've kept journals throughout my life; and now, with Bond being back in my career, maybe I'll find some way to tell these Irish stories in print. There's lots of imagery there which is so richly lyrical, so funny.

I'd really like to direct or produce a love story, a very simple story, with humor. I'm not quite sure what it is at the moment. I'd like to find and produce—not direct, not right now—but I'd like to find a story which means something to me, and get a bunch of actors together and make the film. That is an ambition.

But right now my first priority is to get Bond right. It's a big responsibility in a sense, it scares the heck out of me some days when I think about it; but it's also very exhilarating, it's very do-able. But I've done two days' work on the movie and already I feel useless, I feel redundant, I feel I'm never going to get this together—and yet I've had glowing critiques come back from the powers that be. But being an actor, I don't trust them.

I never saw him again. A lot of garbage happened, some of which I blame myself for, some of which I cannot be responsible for—the media has taken so many things out of context. I was in Thailand when I got the news that my father died—he'd been sick in hospital. I got a letter which arrived very late, and then by the time I began to even contemplate making a move and trying to sort something out, he died.

It's so sad—an unfinished story . . .

ILLUSTRATED INTERVIEWS WITH
gabriel byrne, liam neeson, **pierce brosnan**,
stephen rea, aidan quinn and patrick bergin

PAINTING

I still paint. I started life as a commercial artist. I wasn't good, I don't think I would have got very far in that field, but throughout the years I've painted, done drawings and doodles on scripts. The painting really came out of Cassie's illness. I remember once, at about three o'clock, four o'clock in the morning, my head was just turning with fear—she was beside me, she was getting over chemotherapy, and I was just really angry with the whole thing. I went downstairs and got the paints out, and I thought, I'll paint, I'll put down all this garbage that's in my head, and I just began to paint. And it didn't come up the way I wanted, so I started painting it with my fingers. I've still got these two paintings which I did, which are of faces and very incoherent dark pieces. Then I put the easel up beside our bedroom—we had an office in the bedroom—and I started to paint, and so in the time I took off to be with Cassie I just painted.

And I began to find a kind of vocabulary, my own vocabulary. Instead of black, dark colors, out came bright, primary colors, pretty straightforward. Over the last seven or eight years painting has stayed with me. And I've sold a couple, I've sold two. One's hanging in the Essex House in New York—it's called "Just Four Guys"—and the other one a producer bought; and those two paintings made money that went to cancer research. So I might have an exhibition at some point. I've been asked a few times. But I paint for myself, it's purely a hobby. It came out of a time in my life where there was turmoil and pain, and from it came color and a great joy, and I love it. I have this great dressing room in the studio up in Watford; it's a big, bright, open room, and I've got two canvases hanging up, and the paint stand. Everyone should paint, you live longer—I read that somewhere.

LIFESTYLE

I like the drink, but you do have to look after yourself. I have a trainer in L.A. who's a good mate of mine, and I've worked out with him every day now for seven years. Every day we run five or six miles together, and pump weights, but every now and then I go off and work and that'll fall by the wayside. I try to keep up the regime when I'm away on location; I'll run, eat the right food—and that's very important. We have to take care of this lovely little pearl that we live on, and there's lots of stuff out there that can kill you if you eat it for too long. So in that respect, I try to look after myself.

I used to smoke. I gave up on the very first day of *Remington Steele*—I have smoked since, but I did give up for those five years. I never touched a cigarette. It was really bizarre. I was on the set—packet of Camels, packet of Marlboro, I was armed to the hilt. First shot? "Yes, ready—cough, cough. . . ." I put the cigarette out and then I didn't smoke for the rest of that day, then a week, then a year went by when I didn't smoke. . . . It was great, because I couldn't have done the series otherwise; it's very strenuous doing a twenty-two-hour series, six days a week. But I have gone back and smoked. Especially when you come back to England or Ireland and you have a pint in a pub, it's "Gimme, I'll just have one—ah, this is good . . ."

Wherever I go in the world I go to churches—I just love churches. I love the contentment within them, the peace, the tranquillity, the bizarreness of some of them.

I'm a Catholic, on my own private terms. I'm a Christian, and I love the ritual of any kind of worship—for the right reason, of course.

ILLUSTRATED INTERVIEWS WITH
gabriel byrne, liam neeson, pierce brosnan,
stephen rea, aidan quinn and patrick bergin

PICTURE SOURCES

GABRIEL BYRNE

Cover, pp22, 24 courtesy of Crimson Films; p14 courtesy of Carmel White (Crimson Films); pp15, 16, 21, 27, 38 courtesy of Gabriel Byrne; p20 courtesy of Michaels Wolfe and Tencer PR; pp31, 32, 41 courtesy of Star Stills.

LIAM NEESON

Cover, p47 courtesy of Star Stills, ©United Artists; pp44, 45, 48 courtesy of Kitty Neeson; p49 courtesy of Camera Press, photo by Tom Wargacki; p51 courtesy of Crimson Films; p52 ©Geffen Pictures, photo by Tom Collins, courtesy of Warner Bros.; p56 courtesy of Star Stills; p58 courtesy of *Film Ireland*, ©Universal Studios and Amblin Entertainment; p61 ©Geffen Pictures, courtesy of Warner Bros.; p62 courtesy of Star Stills, ©Universal City Studios and Amblin Entertainment.

AIDAN QUINN

Cover courtesy of Crimson Films; pp66, 67, 68, 71 courtesy of Aidan Quinn and Trixie Flynn; pp73, 80 courtesy of Star Stills; p75 courtesy of Retna Pictures, ©Steve Granitz and Retna Ltd; p76 ©Geffen Pictures, courtesy of Warner Bros.

STEPHEN REA

Cover courtesy of Crimson Films; pp85, 88 courtesy of the Sunday Tribune files; p86 ©Geffen Pictures, photo by David James, courtesy of Warner Bros.;

p90 courtesy of Camera Press, photo by Tom Wargacki; p92 courtesy of Star Stills; pp96, 98 courtesy of Star Stills, ©Polygram Filmed Entertainment.

PATRICK BERGIN

Cover courtesy of Crimson Films; pp102, 104, 105 courtesy of Patrick Bergin/Gerry McColgan/Crimson Films; p107 courtesy of Caroline Dawson Associates; p109 courtesy of Star Stills, ©Twentieth Century Fox; p110 courtesy of Gerry McColgan/Crimson Films, ©Carolco; p113 courtesy of Gerry McColgan, ©Gerry McColgan.

PIERCE BROSNAN

Cover courtesy of Crimson Films; p122, 128, 136 courtesy of Star Stills; p124 courtesy of Retna Pictures, ©Steve Granitz/Retna Ltd; p 127 courtesy of Star Stills, ©Vestron; p131 courtesy of Retna Pictures, ©Bill Davila/Retna Ltd.

ILLUSTRATED INTERVIEWS WITH
gabriel byrne, liam neeson, pierce brosnan,
stephen rea, aidan quinn and patrick bergin

FILMOGRAPHIES

**To Be Released
* Released UK/Ireland

Title	Director
G A B R I E L B Y R N E	
1981	
Excalibur	John Boorman
1983	
The Keep	Michael Mann
Reflections	Kevin Billington
Wagner	Tony Palmer
1984	
Hanna K.	Costa-Gavras
1985	
Defence of the Realm	David Drury
1986	
Gothic	Ken Russell
Lionheart*	Franklin Schaffner
1987	
The Courier*	Frank Deasy
Hello Again	Frank Perry
Julia and Julia	Peter Del Monte
1988	
Diamond Skulls*	Nick Broomfield
Siesta	Mary Lambert
A Soldier's Tale	Larry Parr
1990	
Dark Obsession	Nick Broomfield
Miller's Crossing	Joel Coen
1991	
Shipwrecked	Nils Goup
1992	
Cool World	Ralph Bakshi
Into the West	Mike Newell

1993

A Dangerous Woman	Stephen Gyllenhaal
Point of No Return	John Badham

1994

A Simple Twist of Fate	Gillies MacKinnon
Trial By Jury	Heywood Gould

1995

Frankie Starlight	Michael Lindsay-Hogg
Little Women	Gillian Armstrong
The Usual Suspects	Brian Singer

1996

Dead Man	Jim Jarmusch
Draíocht	Áine O'Connor
*The Last of the High Kings***	David Keating
Mad Dog Time	Larry Bishop

1997

Smilla's Sense of Snow	Billy August
*End of Violence***	Wim Wenders
*The Man in the Iron Mask***	Randall Wallace
*The Polish Wedding***	Teresa Connolly
*The Prince of Jutland**	Gabriel Axel
*This Is the Sea**	Mary McGuckian
*Weapons of Mass Destruction***	Steven Surjik

LIAM NEESON

1981

Excalibur	John Boorman

1983

Krull	Peter Yates

1984

The Bounty	Roger Donaldson
*The Innocent**	John McKenzie

1985

Lamb	Colin Gregg

1986

Duet For One	Andrei Konchalovsky

The Mission	Roland Joffe
Suspect	Peter Yates

1987

High Spirits	Neil Jordan

1988

The Dead Pool	Clint Eastwood
The Good Mother	Leonard Nimoy
Next of Kin	John Irvin
Satisfaction	Joan Freeman

1990

The Big Man	David Leland
Darkman	Sam Raimi

1991

Under Suspicion	Simon Moore

1992

Husbands and Wives	Woody Allen
Leap of Faith	Richard Pearce
Shining Through	David Seltzer

1993

Deception	Graeme Clifford
Ethan Frome	John Madden
Schindler's List	Steven Spielberg

1994

Rob Roy	Michael Caton-Jones

1995

Before and After	Barbet Schroeder
Nell	Michael Apted

1996

Michael Collins	Neil Jordan

AIDAN QUINN

1984

Reckless	James Foley

1985

Desperately Seeking Susan	Susan Seidelman

ILLUSTRATED INTERVIEWS WITH
gabriel byrne, liam neeson, pierce brosnan,
stephen rea, aidan quinn and patrick bergin

1986
The Mission — Roland Joffe

1987
Stakeout — John Badham

1988
Crusoe — Caleb Deschanel

1990
Avalon — Barry Levinson
The Handmaid's Tale — Volker Schlondorff
The Lemon Sisters — Joyce Chopra

1991
At Play in the Fields of the Lord — Hector Babenco
The Playboys — Gillies McKinnon

1993
Benny and Joon — Jeremy Chechik

1994
Blink — Michael Apted
Legends of the Fall — Edward Zwick
Mary Shelley's Frankenstein — Kenneth Branagh

1995
Haunted — Lewis Gilbert
The Stars Fell on Henrietta — James Keach

1996
Looking For Richard — Al Pacino
Michael Collins — Neil Jordan

STEPHEN REA

1982
Angel (US: Danny Boy) — Neil Jordan

1984
Loose Connections — Richard Eyre

1985
The Company of Wolves — Neil Jordan
The Doctor and the Devils — Freddie Francis

1992
The Crying Game — Neil Jordan

1993

Bad Behavior   Les Blair

1994

Angie   Martha Coolidge
Interview With the Vampire   Neil Jordan
Prêt-a-Porter (US: Ready to Wear)   Robert Altman
Princess Caraboo   Michael Austin

1995

Citizen X   Chris Gerolmo
Devil and the Deep Blue Sea*   Marion Hansel

1996

The Last of the High Kings*   David Keating
Michael Collins   Neil Jordan

1997

The Butcher Boy**   Neil Jordan

PATRICK BERGIN

1987

The Courier*   Frank Deasy

1988

Taffin   Francis Megahy

1989

Mountains of the Moon   Bob Rafelson

1991

Highway to Hell   Ate De Jong
Sleeping With the Enemy   Joseph Ruben

1992

Frankenstein   David Wickes
Love Crimes   Lizzie Borden
Map of the Human Heart   Vincent Ward
Patriot Games   Philip Noyce

1993

They (They Watch)   John Korty

1994

Double Cross   Michael Keusch
Soft Deceit   Jorge Montesi

1995

Triplecross   Jeno Hodi

1996

Lawnmower Man 2   Farhad Mann

PIERCE BROSNAN

1979

The Long Good Friday   John Mackenzie

1980

The Mirror Crack'd   Guy Hamilton

1985

Nomads   John McTiernan

1987

The Fourth Protocol   John Macking

1988

The Deceivers   Nicolas Meyer
Taffin   Francis Megahy

1991

Mister Johnson   Bruce Beresford

1992

The Lawnmower Man   Brett Leonard

1993

Mrs. Doubtfire   Chris Columbus

1994

Love Affair   Warren Beatty

1995

Goldeneye   Martin Campbell

1996

Mars Attacks!   Tim Burton
The Mirror Has Two Faces   Barbra Streisand

1997

Dante's Peak   Roger Donaldson